Math in Focus®

Singapore Math®
by Marshall Cavendish

Student Edition

Program Consultant and Author
Dr. Fong Ho Kheong

Authors
Chelvi Ramakrishnan
Michelle Choo

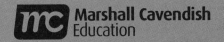
Marshall Cavendish
Education

U.S. Distributor

Houghton Mifflin Harcourt.
The Learning Company™

Grade
3B

Contents

Chapter

7 Fractions

Hands-on Activity

8 Measurement

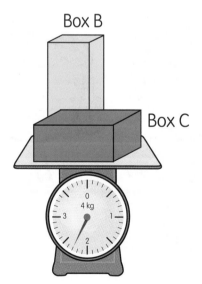

Box B

Box C

1 L

500 mL

Area and Perimeter

Chapter Opener   113

 What is the relationship between area and perimeter?

RECALL PRIOR KNOWLEDGE   114

Multiplying using an area model • Showing a shape
on dot paper and on grid paper • Measuring length
using metric units • Measuring length using customary units
• Measuring lengths with a ruler

🔵 Hands-on Activity

© 2020 Marshall Cavendish Education Pte Ltd

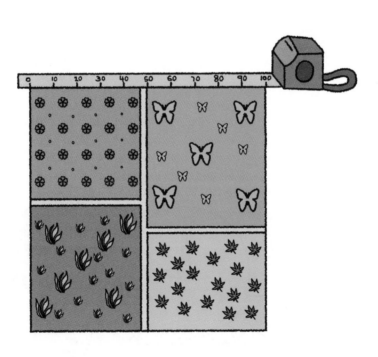

Chapter

10 Time

Chapter Opener

11 Graphs and Line Plots

Chapter Opener

 How can you organize data?

RECALL PRIOR KNOWLEDGE

Using graphs to show data

▶ Hands-on Activity

Number of Butterflies Seen

Juan	🦋🦋🦋🦋	4
Kylie	🦋🦋🦋🦋🦋🦋🦋🦋🦋🦋	10
Irene	🦋🦋🦋🦋🦋🦋🦋🦋	8
Caleb	🦋🦋🦋🦋🦋🦋	6

Key: Each 🦋 stands for 1 butterfly.

Chapter

12 Angles, Lines, and Two-Dimensional Figures

Manipulative List

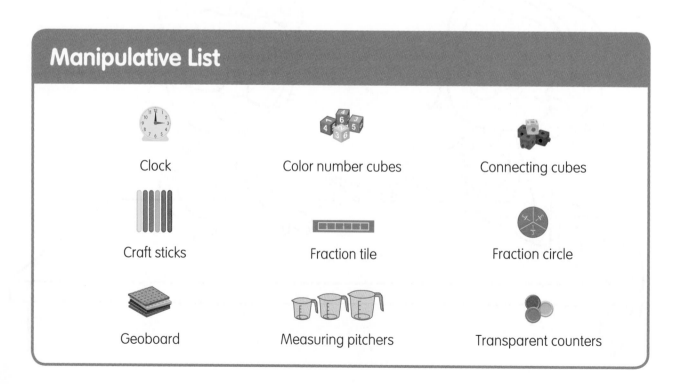

Clock

Color number cubes

Connecting cubes

Craft sticks

Fraction tile

Fraction circle

Geoboard

Measuring pitchers

Transparent counters

Preface

Welcome!

Math in Focus® is a program that puts **you** at the center of an exciting learning experience! This experience is all about helping you to build skills and math ideas that make sense, sharing your thinking to deepen your understanding, and learning to become a strong and confident problem solver!

What's in your book?

Each chapter in this book begins with a real-world example of the math topic you are about to learn.

In each chapter, you will see the following features:

THINK introduces a problem for the whole section, to get you thinking creatively and critically. You may not be able to answer the problem right away but you can come back to it a few times as you work through the section.

ENGAGE introduces tasks that link what you already know with what you will be learning next. The tasks will have you exploring and discussing math concepts with your classmates.

LEARN introduces you to new math concepts through a Concrete-Pictorial-Abstract (C-P-A) approach, using examples and activities.

Hands-on Activity provides you with the experience of working very closely with your classmates. These Hands-On Activities allow you to become more confident in what you have learned and help you to uncover new concepts.

TRY provides you with the opportunity to practice what you are learning, with support and guidance.

INDEPENDENT PRACTICE allows you to work on different kinds of problems and apply the concepts and skills you have learned to solve these problems on your own.

Additional features include:

RECALL PRIOR KNOWLEDGE	Math Talk	MATH SHARING	GAME
Helps you recall related concepts you learned before, accompanied by practice questions	Invites you to explain your reasoning and communicate your ideas to your classmates and teachers	Encourages you to create strategies, discover methods, and share them with your classmates and teachers using mathematical language	Helps you to really master the concepts you learned, through fun partner games
LET'S EXPLORE	**MATH JOURNAL**	**PUT ON YOUR THINKING CAP!**	**CHAPTER WRAP-UP**
Extends your learning through investigation	Allows you to reflect on your learning when you write down your thoughts about the concepts learned	Challenges you to apply the concepts to solve problems in different ways	Summarizes your learning in a flow chart and helps you to make connections within the chapter
CHAPTER REVIEW	**Assessment Prep**	**PERFORMANCE TASK**	**STEAM**
Provides you with a lot of practice in the concepts learned	Prepares you for state tests with assessment-type problems	Assesses your learning through problems that allow you to demonstrate your understanding and knowledge	Promotes collaboration with your classmates through interesting projects that allow you to use math in creative ways

Let's begin your exciting learning journey with us! Are you ready?

Chapter 7

Fractions

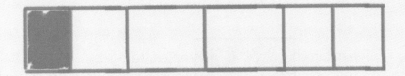

$\frac{1}{4}$ of my paper is colored.

Is $\frac{1}{4}$ of my paper colored too?

How can you find equivalent fractions?

Dividing shapes into equal parts

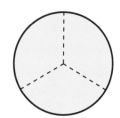 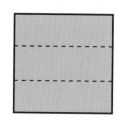

These shapes are divided into 2 halves.

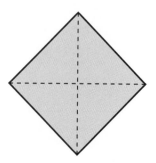 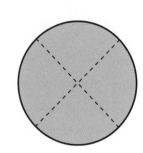

These shapes are divided into 3 thirds.

These shapes are divided into 4 fourths.

▶ **Quick Check**

Draw line(s) to divide each shape equally.

1. 2 halves

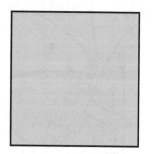 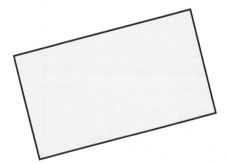

2 3 thirds

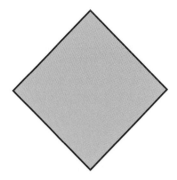
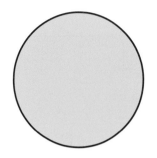

3 4 fourths

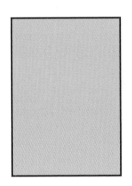

Representing numbers on a number line

You can use a number line to show numbers.

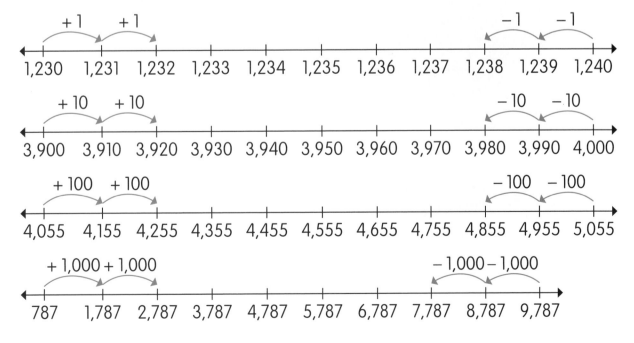

▶ **Quick Check**

Find each missing number.

4
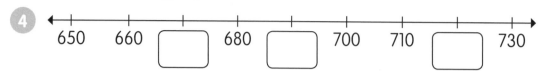
650　660　☐　680　☐　700　710　☐　730

5
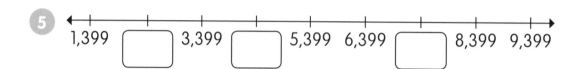
1,399　☐　3,399　☐　5,399　6,399　☐　8,399　9,399

6

7,204　7,205　☐　7,207　7,208　☐　☐　7,211　7,212

7
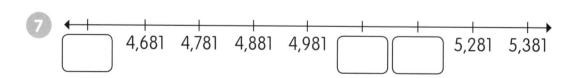
☐　4,681　4,781　4,881　4,981　☐　☐　5,281　5,381

Understanding Unit Fractions

Learning Objectives:
- Read, write, and identify unit fractions for halves, thirds, fourths, sixths, and eighths.
- Show fractions and wholes using fraction models.

New Vocabulary
fraction
whole
numerator
denominator
unit fraction

THINK

Adrian has a triangle with equal sides.
How can he divide the triangle into equal parts?

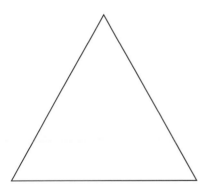

ENGAGE

a   Divide a piece of paper into two equal parts.
What do you call one part?

b   Now, divide the same piece of paper into four equal parts.
What do you call one part?

c   Next, divide the piece of paper into eight equal parts.
Do you notice a pattern?
Explain your thinking to your partner.

LEARN Use fractions to describe equal parts of a whole

1. This is a pie.
It is one whole.

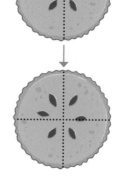

Mía cuts the pie into 2 equal parts.
Each part is one half of the pie.
You can write one-half as $\frac{1}{2}$.
$\frac{1}{2}$ is 1 out of 2 equal parts.

Mía cuts the pie further into 4 equal parts.
Each part is one fourth of the pie.
You can write one-fourth as $\frac{1}{4}$.
$\frac{1}{4}$ is 1 out of 4 equal parts.

$\frac{1}{2}$ and $\frac{1}{4}$ are examples of fractions.

A fraction is a number that names equal parts of a whole.
A whole describes a complete figure and is equal to 1.

$$\frac{1}{2} \begin{array}{l} \rightarrow \text{numerator} \\ \rightarrow \text{denominator} \end{array}$$

The numerator shows the number of equal part(s) of the whole that is shaded.

The denominator shows the number of equal part(s) the whole is divided into.

Math Talk

How can you divide the rectangle into 3 equal parts?
What fraction of the rectangle is each part?

2 How do you read fractional parts?

Fraction	Read as
$\frac{1}{2}$	one-half
$\frac{1}{3}$	one-third
$\frac{1}{4}$	one-fourth or one-quarter
$\frac{1}{6}$	one-sixth
$\frac{1}{8}$	one-eighth

$\frac{1}{2}, \frac{1}{3}, \frac{1}{4}, \frac{1}{6}$, and $\frac{1}{8}$ are unit fractions.
A unit fraction names one of the equal parts of a whole.

3 This rectangle shows a whole with 2 equal parts.

1 part is red and 1 part is blue.

The red part is $\frac{1}{2}$ of the whole.

1 part + 1 part = 2 parts or 1 whole
Number of red parts = 1
Total number of parts in the whole = 2

The blue part is $\frac{1}{2}$ of the whole.

The red part and the blue part make one whole.
$\frac{1}{2}$ and $\frac{1}{2}$ make 1 whole.

© 2020 Marshall Cavendish Education Pte Ltd

Hands-on Activity — Using fractions to describe equal parts of a whole

Work in pairs.

Your teacher will provide you with five rectangular strips of paper.

(1) Fold a rectangular strip of paper into 2 equal parts.

(2) Shade one of the equal parts.
What fraction of the whole is the shaded part?

The shaded part is $\dfrac{\Box}{\Box}$ of the whole.

(3) Repeat (1) and (2) using the remaining strips of paper with the following number of equal parts.

    a   3 equal parts

       The shaded part is $\dfrac{\Box}{\Box}$ of the whole.

    b   4 equal parts

       The shaded part is $\dfrac{\Box}{\Box}$ of the whole.

    c   6 equal parts

       The shaded part is $\dfrac{\Box}{\Box}$ of the whole.

    d   8 equal parts

       The shaded part is $\dfrac{\Box}{\Box}$ of the whole.

Name: _____ Date: _____

2 Fractions as Part of a Whole

Learning Objectives:
- Represent fractions using fraction circles and tiles.
- Read, write, and identify fractions of a whole.
- Show fractions as points or distances on a number line.
- Express whole numbers as fractions.

THINK

One whole can be divided into many equal parts.
How can you write one whole as a fraction in three different ways?

ENGAGE

a   Use  to show that 4 fourths make a whole.

Take 3 parts. What fraction of the whole did you take?

b   Can the following diagram be used to show the fraction?
Explain your thinking to your partner.

LEARN Use models to show fractions as part of a whole

1 Maria divides a rectangle into 4 equal parts.

3 out of 4 parts are orange.
$\frac{3}{4}$ of the rectangle is orange.
$\frac{3}{4}$ is read as three-fourths.
$\frac{3}{4} = \frac{1}{4} + \frac{1}{4} + \frac{1}{4}$

1 out of 4 parts is white.
$\frac{1}{4}$ of the rectangle is white.
$\frac{3}{4}$ and $\frac{1}{4}$ make 1 whole.

Hands-on Activity Using models to show fractions as part of a whole

Work in groups.

Your teacher will provide you with a part of a .

1. Form groups with your classmates to make a whole with your .

2. Draw and divide a circle into the parts formed by your group. Write a sentence for the number of parts that make 1 whole.

3. Color a few parts. Write two sentences to describe the colored parts in fractions.

Math Talk

What fraction of the rectangle is not shaded?

TRY Practice using models to show fractions as part of a whole

Write down the fraction of each model that is shaded.

1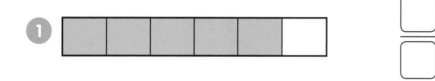
$$\frac{\boxed{}}{\boxed{}}$$

2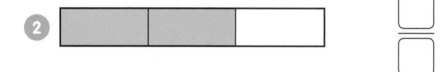
$$\frac{\boxed{}}{\boxed{}}$$

3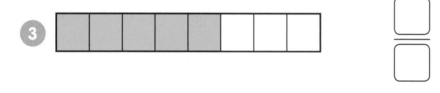
$$\frac{\boxed{}}{\boxed{}}$$

4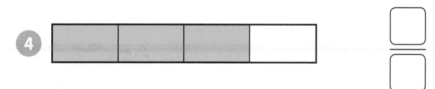
$$\frac{\boxed{}}{\boxed{}}$$

Shade the model to show each fraction.
Then, fill in each box.

5 $\frac{2}{3}$

$\frac{2}{3} = \dfrac{\boxed{}}{\boxed{}} + \dfrac{\boxed{}}{\boxed{}}$

$\frac{2}{3}$ and $\dfrac{\boxed{}}{\boxed{}}$ make 1 whole.

6 $\frac{3}{8}$

$\frac{3}{8} = \dfrac{\boxed{}}{\boxed{}} + \dfrac{\boxed{}}{\boxed{}} + \dfrac{\boxed{}}{\boxed{}}$

$\frac{3}{8}$ and $\dfrac{\boxed{}}{\boxed{}}$ make 1 whole.

ENGAGE

a Divide a bar into 2 equal parts.

What is the fraction of each part?

b Draw a number line with 0 and 1 as the endpoints.

Mark (✗) and label $\frac{1}{2}$ on your number line.

c Draw a fraction model and a number line to show $\frac{2}{3}$.

Share how you did it with your partner.

LEARN Show fractions on a number line

1 Number lines can be used to show fractions.

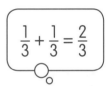

$\frac{1}{3} + \frac{1}{3} = \frac{2}{3}$

The interval between 0 and 1 represents 1 whole.

It is divided into 3 equal parts.

Each part is $\frac{1}{3}$.

2 You can also show fractions greater than 1 whole on a number line.

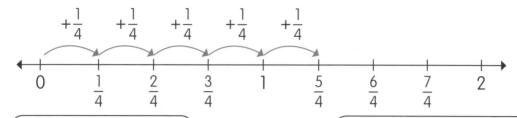

$$\frac{1}{4} + \frac{1}{4} + \frac{1}{4} + \frac{1}{4} + \frac{1}{4} = \frac{5}{4}$$

1 whole $= \frac{1}{4} + \frac{1}{4} + \frac{1}{4} + \frac{1}{4}$

$= \frac{4}{4}$

2 wholes $= \frac{8}{4}$

TRY Practice showing fractions on a number line

Fill in each blank.
Use the number line to help you.

1
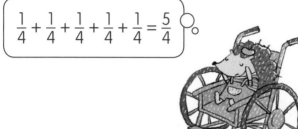

2
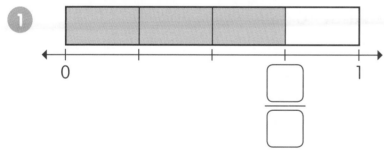

3
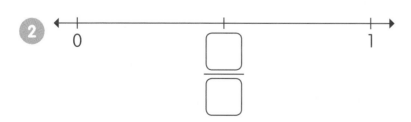

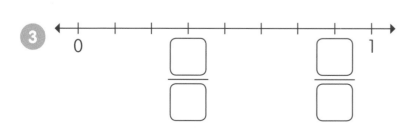

Make an **X** to show each fraction on the number line.

4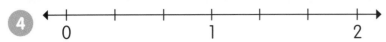

    a $\dfrac{1}{3}$ **b** $\dfrac{4}{3}$

5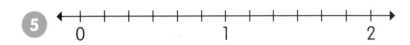

    a $\dfrac{4}{6}$ **b** $\dfrac{7}{6}$ **c** $\dfrac{11}{6}$

ENGAGE

1 Draw a circle and divide it into 5 equal parts.
Shade 1 part. What fraction of the whole is shaded?
Now, shade 1 more part.
What fraction of the whole is shaded now?
Do you see a pattern? What fraction represents the circle
when all 5 parts are shaded?

2 Draw a bar model and divide it into 8 equal parts.
What fraction represents the bar when all the parts
are shaded?
Explain your thinking to your partner.

3 Draw 2 circles and divide each circle into 4 equal parts.
If all 4 parts of each circle are shaded, what fraction
represents the total number of shaded parts?
Explain your thinking to your partner.

LEARN Express whole numbers as fractions

1. The whole is divided into 1 part.
You can write 1 whole as $\frac{1}{1}$.

 1 whole = $\frac{1}{1}$

> The numerator tells you the number of equal parts you have.
> The denominator tells you the number of equal parts a whole is divided into.

 2 wholes = $\frac{2}{1}$

 3 wholes = $\frac{3}{1}$

TRY Practice expressing whole numbers as fractions

Express each of the following as a fraction.

1. 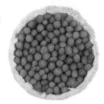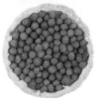 3 wholes = $\frac{\Box}{\Box}$

2.
 4 wholes = $\frac{\Box}{\Box}$

FRACTIONS MATCH UP!

What you need:

Players: 2 to 3
Materials: Fraction cards (Set A), Fraction model cards (Set B)

What to do:

1. Shuffle each set of cards and arrange them face down on the table.

2. Player 1 flips over a card from each deck. If the fraction matches the fraction model, he or she gets to keep the pair of cards. Player 1 then gets another turn.

3. If the fraction does not match the fraction model, the game moves on to the next player until there are no more cards left on the table.

Who is the winner?

The player with the most cards wins.

Name: _____ Date: _____

INDEPENDENT PRACTICE

Fill in each blank.

The whole is divided into _____ equal parts.

_____ out of _____ parts are shaded.

$\dfrac{\square}{\square}$ of the whole is shaded.

$\dfrac{\square}{\square}$ of the whole is not shaded.

2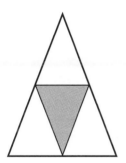

The whole is divided into _____ equal parts.

_____ out of _____ parts are shaded.

$\dfrac{\square}{\square}$ of the whole is shaded.

$\dfrac{\square}{\square}$ of the whole is not shaded.

3

The whole is divided into _____ equal parts.

_____ out of _____ parts are shaded.

$\frac{\boxed{}}{\boxed{}}$ of the whole is shaded.

$\frac{\boxed{}}{\boxed{}}$ of the whole is not shaded.

4

The whole is divided into _____ equal parts.

_____ out of _____ parts are shaded.

$\frac{\boxed{}}{\boxed{}}$ of the whole is shaded.

$\frac{\boxed{}}{\boxed{}}$ of the whole is not shaded.

Fill in each missing fraction.

5

$\frac{1}{8}$ and $\frac{\boxed{}}{\boxed{}}$ make 1 whole.

6

$\frac{5}{6}$ and $\frac{\boxed{}}{\boxed{}}$ make 1 whole.

Fill in each blank on the number line.

7

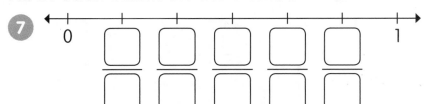

8

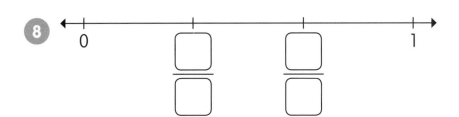

Make an **✗** and label each fraction on the number line.

9

a $\dfrac{2}{3}$

b $\dfrac{5}{3}$

10

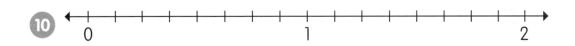

a $\dfrac{6}{8}$

b $\dfrac{11}{8}$

c $\dfrac{13}{8}$

11

a $\dfrac{2}{4}$

b $\dfrac{7}{4}$

c $\dfrac{11}{4}$

Express each of the following as a fraction.

12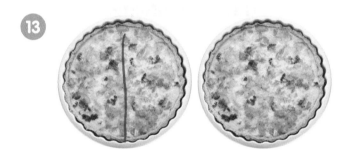

4 wholes = $\dfrac{4}{4}$

13

2 wholes = $\dfrac{1}{2}$

14

3 wholes = $\dfrac{3}{?}$

3 Fractions as Part of a Set

Learning Objectives:
- Read, write, and identify fractions of a set.
- Find the number of items in a fraction of a set.

THINK

$\frac{3}{8}$ of the students in a class wear glasses.

9 students in the class wear glasses.
How many students are there in the class?

ENGAGE

1. Take 1 ▪ and 2 ▪.
   What fraction of the cubes are red?

2. Ariana has 7 ▪ and some ▪ covered under a cup.
   There are fewer ▪ than ▪.
   What fraction of the cubes are red?
   List all the possible fractions.

LEARN Use pictures to show fractions as part of a set

1. There are 3 apples.

   2 out of the 3 apples are red.
   $\frac{2}{3}$ of the apples are red.

   1 out of the 3 apples is green.
   $\frac{1}{3}$ of the apples are green.

   $\frac{2}{3}$ → number of red apples
   $\phantom{\frac{2}{3}}$ → total number of apples

   $\frac{1}{3}$ → number of green apples
   $\phantom{\frac{1}{3}}$ → total number of apples

2 There are 9 apples.
The apples are divided into 3 equal groups.

2 out of 3 equal groups of apples are red.
$\frac{2}{3}$ of the apples are red.

1 out of 3 equal groups of apples is green.
$\frac{1}{3}$ of the apples are green.

3	3	3

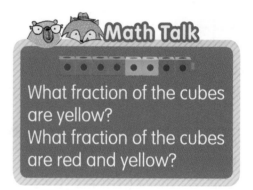

Math Talk

What fraction of the cubes are yellow?
What fraction of the cubes are red and yellow?

TRY Practice using pictures to show fractions as part of a set

Divide the circles into equal groups.
Then, fill in each blank.

1

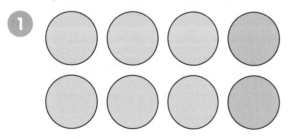

$\dfrac{\square}{\square}$ of the circles are blue.

$\dfrac{\square}{\square}$ of the circles are green.

ENGAGE

There are 12 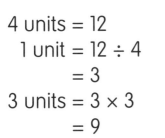 and ⬜. $\frac{1}{3}$ of the cubes are blue.

Draw a bar model to represent this information.

Explain how you can find the number of 🟦 to your partner.

LEARN Use bar models to show fractions as part of a set

1　Ms. White had 12 oranges.

She gave $\frac{3}{4}$ of the oranges to Cooper.

How many oranges did she give to Cooper?

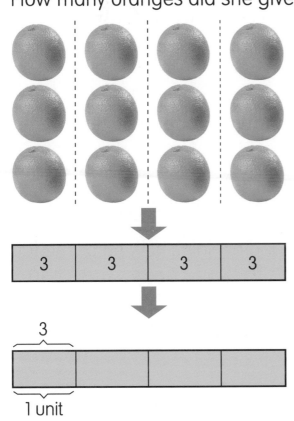

Put the oranges into 4 equal groups.
Each group represents $\frac{1}{4}$ of the oranges.

| 3 | 3 | 3 | 3 |

⬇

1 unit

4 units = 12

1 unit = 12 ÷ 4

= 3

3 units = 3 × 3

= 9

She gave Cooper 9 oranges.

2 Find $\frac{5}{8}$ of 24.

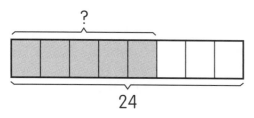

24

Draw a bar model.
Divide it into 8 equal parts.
Shade 5 parts.

8 units = 24
1 unit = 24 ÷ 8
        = 3
5 units = 3 × 5
        = 15

So, $\frac{5}{8}$ of 24 is 15.

Hands-on Activity Using ⬤ to show a fraction of a set

Work in pairs.

1 Count 12 ⬤.

2 Your partner shows $\frac{2}{3}$ of 12 ⬤ and explains how he or she found the answer.

Example:
I divide the counters into 3 equal groups.
$\frac{2}{3}$ is 2 out of 3 equal groups.
There are 8 counters in 2 groups.

3 Trade places. Repeat ① and ② for the following.

a $\frac{1}{4}$ of 16

b $\frac{5}{6}$ of 24

TRY Practice using bar models to show fractions as part of a set

Check (✓) the correct set.

1 Which of the following sets shows $\frac{3}{8}$ of it shaded?

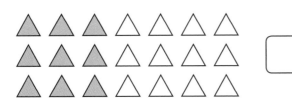 □

 □

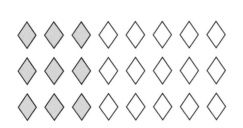 □

 □

Solve.

2 Find $\frac{2}{3}$ of 18.

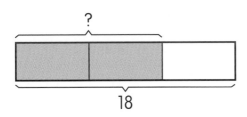

18

3 units = _____

1 unit = _____ ◯ _____

= _____

2 units = _____ ◯ _____

= _____

So, $\frac{2}{3}$ of 18 is _____.

3 Find $\frac{1}{2}$ of 22.

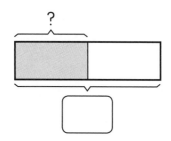

Find the value of each of the following.
Draw a bar model to help you.

4 $\frac{7}{8}$ of 16

5 $\frac{3}{4}$ of 20

Name: _Kaylee. T_   Date: _____

INDEPENDENT PRACTICE

Solve.

1 What fraction of the rectangles are yellow?

$\dfrac{3}{7}$ of the rectangles are yellow.

2 What fraction of the circles are blue?

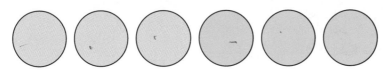

$\dfrac{3}{6}$ of the circles are blue.

3 What fraction of the stars are red?

$\dfrac{2}{8}$ of the stars are red.

Use the pictures to help you answer each question.

4

$\frac{1}{2}$ of 6 = _____

$\frac{1}{3}$ of 6 = _____

$\frac{1}{6}$ of 6 = _____

5

$\frac{1}{2}$ of 8 = _____

$\frac{1}{4}$ of 8 = _____

$\frac{1}{8}$ of 8 = _____

6

$\frac{1}{2}$ of 12 = _____

$\frac{1}{3}$ of 12 = _____

$\frac{1}{4}$ of 12 = _____

$\frac{1}{6}$ of 12 = _____

Shade to show each fraction.

7 $\frac{1}{4}$

8 $\frac{3}{8}$

9 $\frac{2}{3}$

Find the value of each of the following.
Draw a bar model to help you.

10 $\frac{5}{6}$ of 24

11 $\frac{3}{4}$ of 16

12 $\frac{1}{3}$ of 18

4 Understanding Equivalent Fractions

Learning Objectives:
- Use models to identify equivalent fractions.
- Use number lines to identify equivalent fractions.

> **New Vocabulary**
> equivalent fractions

THINK

Write three equivalent fractions using all the numbers 3, 4, 6, 8, 15, and 20.

ENGAGE

Use  to show $\frac{1}{2}$, $\frac{2}{4}$, and $\frac{4}{8}$.

What do you notice? Share your ideas with your partner.

LEARN Find equivalent fractions

① Andrea, Henry, and Kiri each have a mini pie of the same size.

Andrea cuts her pie into 2 equal parts.
She eats 1 part out of the 2 equal parts.
She eats $\frac{1}{2}$ of her pie.

$\frac{1}{2}$

Henry cuts his pie into 4 equal parts.
He eats 2 parts out of the 4 equal parts.
He eats $\frac{2}{4}$ of his pie.

$\frac{2}{4}$

Kiri cuts his pie into 6 equal parts.
He eats 3 parts out of the 6 equal parts.
He eats $\frac{3}{6}$ of his pie.

$\frac{3}{6}$

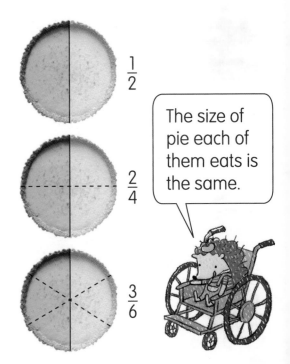

> The size of pie each of them eats is the same.

$\frac{1}{2}$, $\frac{2}{4}$, and $\frac{3}{6}$ are equivalent fractions.

2 You can use number lines to find equivalent fractions.

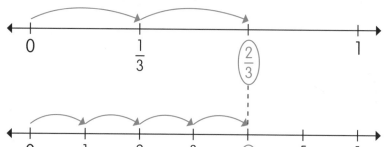

$\dfrac{2}{3}$ and $\dfrac{4}{6}$ are equivalent fractions.

$$\dfrac{2}{3} = \dfrac{4}{6}$$

Hands-on Activity Finding equivalent fractions

1 Use 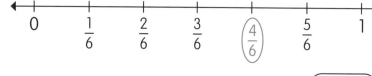 or ▭ to find an equivalent fraction of $\dfrac{1}{4}$.

2 Show the equivalent fractions on the number lines below.

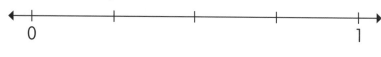

3 Repeat **1** and **2** for the following.

a $\dfrac{2}{4}$ b $\dfrac{3}{4}$

Practice finding equivalent fractions

Find each equivalent fraction.

1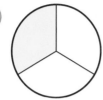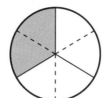

$$\frac{1}{3} \quad = \quad \frac{\square}{\square}$$

2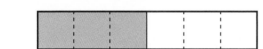

$$\frac{1}{2} = \frac{\square}{\square}$$

Shade to show each fraction.
Then, find the equivalent fractions.

3

$$\frac{6}{8} \qquad \frac{4}{6} \qquad \frac{3}{4} \qquad \frac{2}{3}$$

$$\frac{\square}{\square} = \frac{\square}{\square} \quad \text{and} \quad \frac{\square}{\square} = \frac{\square}{\square}$$

Find each equivalent fraction.
Use the empty model to help you.

 $\dfrac{2}{8}$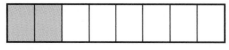

$$\dfrac{2}{8} = \dfrac{\square}{\square}$$

5 $\dfrac{2}{6}$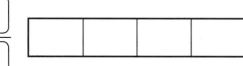

$$\dfrac{2}{6} = \dfrac{\square}{\square}$$

Use the number lines to find the equivalent fractions.

6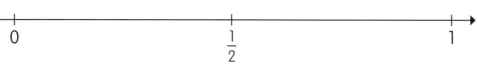

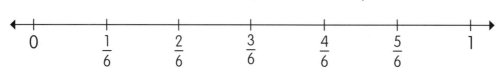

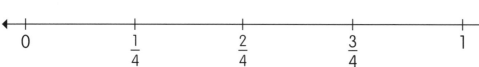

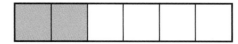

$$\dfrac{\square}{2} = \dfrac{2}{\square} = \dfrac{\square}{6} = \dfrac{4}{\square}$$

Name: _____   Date: _____

INDEPENDENT PRACTICE

Write the fraction of each model that is shaded.
Then, match the equivalent fractions.

1

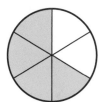 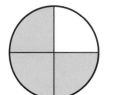 ·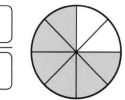

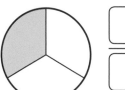 ·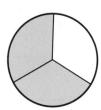

 ·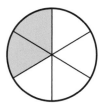

Shade each model to show the given fraction.
Then, check (✓) the boxes beside the two equivalent fractions.

2 $\frac{6}{6}$ 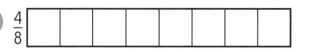 ☐

$\frac{3}{6}$  ☐

$\frac{2}{4}$ ☐

3 $\frac{4}{8}$ 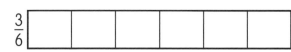 ☐

$\frac{3}{8}$ ☐

$\frac{3}{6}$ ☐

© 2020 Marshall Cavendish Education Pte Ltd

Fill in each missing fraction on the number lines.
Then, write the equivalent fractions.

4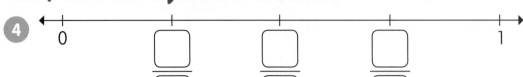

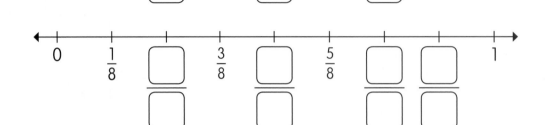

$$\frac{1}{4} = \frac{\boxed{}}{\boxed{}} \qquad \frac{\boxed{}}{4} = \frac{4}{\boxed{}} \qquad \frac{3}{\boxed{}} = \frac{\boxed{}}{8}$$

5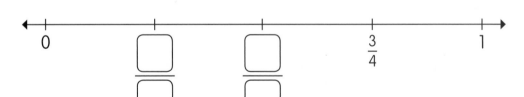

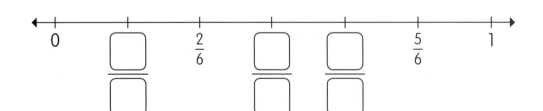

$$\frac{\boxed{}}{2} = \frac{\boxed{}}{\boxed{}} = \frac{\boxed{}}{\boxed{}}$$

 **Comparing Fractions**

Learning Objective:
• Compare fractions using models of the same size.

New Vocabulary
like fractions

THINK

Fernando writes four fractions in sequence: $\frac{1}{4}$, A, $\frac{5}{8}$, B
What are the possible fractions that A and B can be?

ENGAGE

1 Use  to show $\frac{3}{8}$ and $\frac{5}{8}$.

   Which fraction is greater? Which is less?

2 Draw bar models to find the greater fraction between $\frac{5}{6}$ and $\frac{3}{4}$.

LEARN Compare fractions

1 Which is greater, $\frac{1}{4}$ or $\frac{3}{4}$?

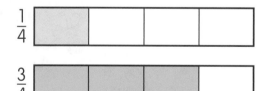

$\frac{3}{4}$ is greater than $\frac{1}{4}$.
$\frac{3}{4} > \frac{1}{4}$

$\frac{1}{4}$ and $\frac{3}{4}$ have the same denominator.
They are called like fractions.
The greater fraction is the one with the greater numerator.

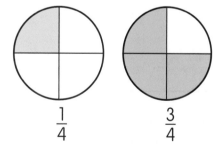

2 Which is less, $\frac{1}{6}$ or $\frac{1}{4}$?

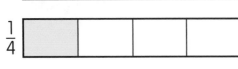

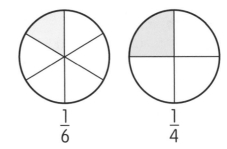

$\frac{1}{6}$
$\frac{1}{4}$

$\frac{1}{6}$ is less than $\frac{1}{4}$.

$\frac{1}{6} < \frac{1}{4}$

$\frac{1}{6}$ and $\frac{1}{4}$ are fractions with the same numerator. The lesser fraction is the one with the greater denominator.

3 Which is less, $\frac{5}{6}$ or $\frac{5}{8}$?

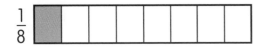

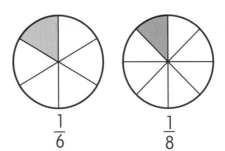

$\frac{1}{6}$
$\frac{1}{8}$

Compare the fractions. Which is less, $\frac{1}{6}$ or $\frac{1}{8}$? Why?

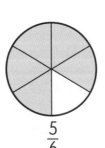

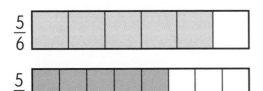

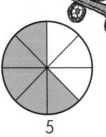

$\frac{5}{6}$
$\frac{5}{8}$

$\frac{5}{8}$ is less than $\frac{5}{6}$.

$\frac{5}{8} < \frac{5}{6}$

Since $\frac{5}{6}$ and $\frac{5}{8}$ have the same numerator, the lesser fraction is the one with the greater denominator.

Activity 1   Finding the lesser fraction

Which fraction is less?

Use 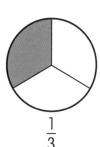 to find out. Circle your answer.

Example:

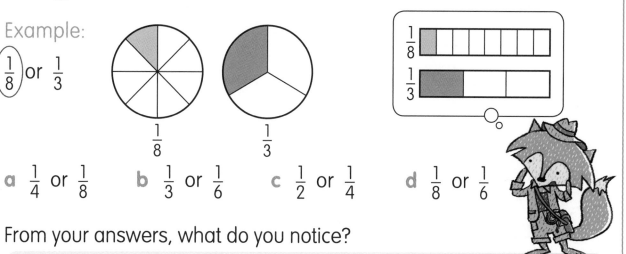

$\left(\dfrac{1}{8}\right)$ or $\dfrac{1}{3}$

a $\dfrac{1}{4}$ or $\dfrac{1}{8}$ b $\dfrac{1}{3}$ or $\dfrac{1}{6}$ c $\dfrac{1}{2}$ or $\dfrac{1}{4}$ d $\dfrac{1}{8}$ or $\dfrac{1}{6}$

From your answers, what do you notice?

Activity 2   Finding the greater fraction

Which fraction is greater?

Use 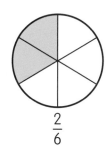 to find out. Circle your answer.

Example:

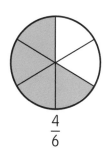

$\dfrac{2}{6}$ or $\left(\dfrac{4}{6}\right)$

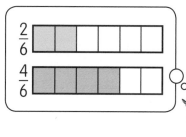

a $\dfrac{2}{3}$ or $\dfrac{1}{3}$ b $\dfrac{2}{4}$ or $\dfrac{3}{4}$ c $\dfrac{7}{8}$ or $\dfrac{5}{8}$ d $\dfrac{5}{6}$ or $\dfrac{3}{6}$

From your answers, what do you notice?

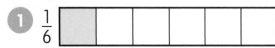 Practice comparing fractions

Compare each pair of fractions. Write < or >.

1. $\frac{1}{6}$

   $\frac{5}{6}$

   $\frac{1}{6}\ \bigcirc\ \frac{5}{6}$

2. $\frac{7}{8}$

   $\frac{3}{8}$

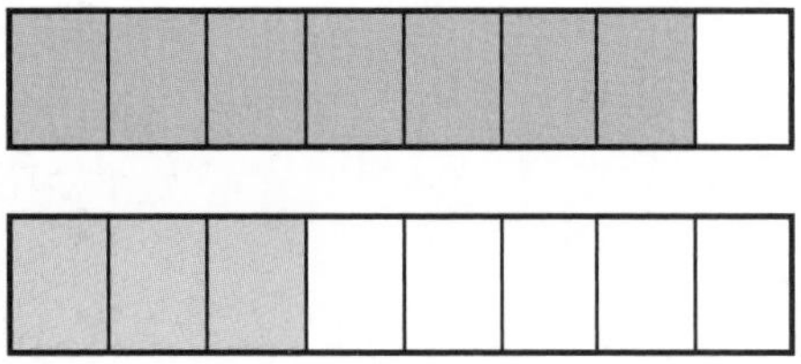

   $\frac{7}{8}\ \bigcirc\ \frac{3}{8}$

3. $\frac{1}{2}$

   $\frac{1}{6}$

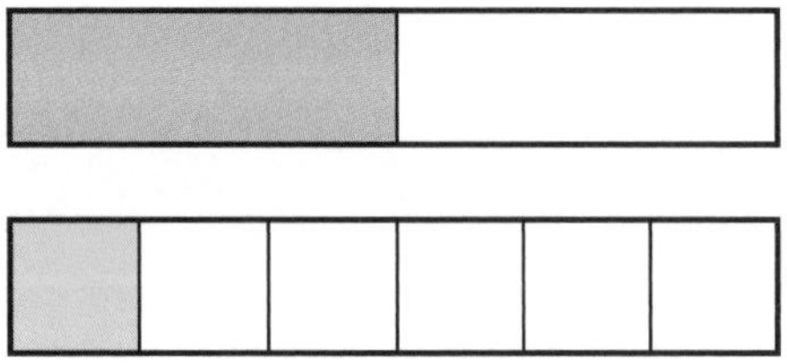

   $\frac{1}{2}\ \bigcirc\ \frac{1}{6}$

4. $\frac{3}{8}$

   $\frac{3}{4}$

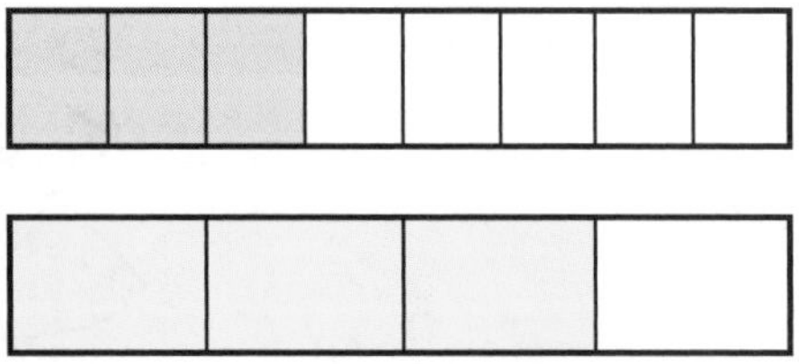

   $\frac{3}{8}\ \bigcirc\ \frac{3}{4}$

THE GREATER THE BETTER!

What you need:

Players: 2
Materials: Fraction comparison cards

What to do:

1. Divide the fraction cards equally among each player.

2. Each player flips over one card and compares the fractions on the cards. The player who points out the card with the greater fraction first gets 1 point.

3. Repeat until both players use up their cards.

Who is the winner?

The player with the most points wins.

Whole numbers can be written as fractions.

The number 1 can be written as $\frac{1}{1}$.
It can also be written as $\frac{2}{2}$.

 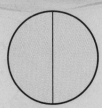

$1 = \frac{1}{1}$ $1 = \frac{2}{2}$

1 What is another fraction for 1?

The number 2 can be written as $\frac{2}{1}$.
It can also be written as $\frac{4}{2}$.

 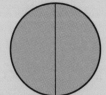

$2 = \frac{2}{1}$ $2 = \frac{4}{2}$

2 What is another fraction for 2?

3 What are two fractions for 5?

4 What number does $\frac{12}{3}$ represent?

Name: _____   Date: _____

Mathematical Habit **2** Use mathematical reasoning

Farmer Nathan has a total of 24 goats and cows.

$\frac{7}{8}$ of them are goats and the rest are cows.

How can you find the number of goats he has?

Order the steps from 1 to 4.

◯ There are 8 units in all.
8 units = 24

◯ There are 7 units of goats.
7 units = 3 × 7
            = 21

He has 21 goats.

◯ I can draw a bar model to show $\frac{7}{8}$.

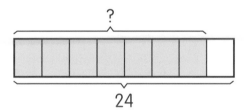

◯ I can find the number of animals each unit represents.
1 unit = 24 ÷ 8
          = 3

Problem Solving with Heuristics

1 **Mathematical Habit 4** Use mathematical models

Joycelyn draws and colors some circles on a piece of paper.

She colors $\frac{1}{3}$ of the circles pink and $\frac{1}{6}$ of the circles blue.

The remaining 12 circles are colored orange.
How many pink circles and blue circles does she draw?
Use a model to help you solve the question.

2 **Mathematical Habit 1** **Persevere in solving problems**

Morgan, Kanda, and Hayden shared a pie.
The pie was cut into 8 equal slices.
Morgan ate $\frac{1}{8}$ of the pie.
Kanda ate more pie than Hayden.
Together, they finished the whole pie.

a   What are some possible fractions that show the parts of the pie Kanda and Hayden each ate?

b   What is the greatest fraction of the pie that Hayden could have eaten?

CHAPTER WRAP-UP

Fractions

Understanding Unit Fractions

A unit fraction names one of the equal parts in a whole.

numerator ← $\frac{1}{8}$ → denominator is one-eighth

The numerator shows the number of equal part(s) of the whole that is required.

The denominator shows the number of equal part(s) the whole is divided into.

Fractions as Part of a Whole

A fraction can show a part of a whole.

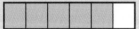

$\frac{5}{6}$ of the rectangle is shaded.

$\frac{1}{6}$ of the rectangle is not shaded.

$\frac{5}{6} + \frac{1}{6} = 1$ whole

1 whole = $\frac{1}{1}$ 2 wholes = $\frac{2}{1}$

Fractions as Part of a Set

A fraction can show a part of a set of objects.

$\frac{2}{3}$ of the stars are blue.

$\frac{1}{3}$ of the stars are pink.

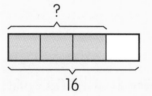

16

4 units = 16
1 unit = 16 ÷ 4 = 4
3 units = 4 × 3 = 12

Understanding Equivalent Fractions

Equivalent fractions show the same part of a whole.

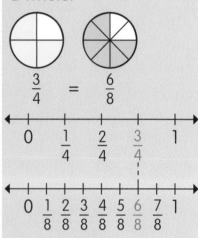

$\frac{3}{4} = \frac{6}{8}$

Comparing Fractions

You can use models to compare fractions.

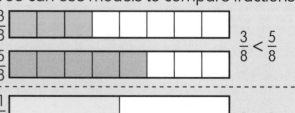

$\frac{3}{8} < \frac{5}{8}$

$\frac{1}{2} > \frac{1}{3}$

Name: _____ Date: _____

Answer each question.

 What fraction of each shape is not shaded?

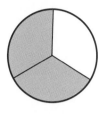 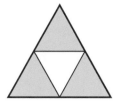 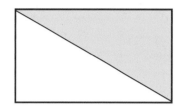

2 What fraction of each shape is shaded?

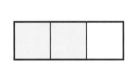 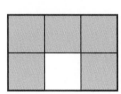 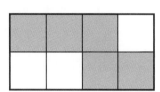

Fill in each missing fraction.

3

   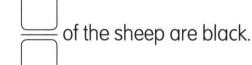
of the sheep are white.

of the sheep are black.

Find the value of each of the following.
Draw a bar model to help you.

④ Find $\frac{1}{4}$ of 20.

⑤ Find $\frac{3}{8}$ of 16.

Make an ✗ on the box that is not true.

⑥
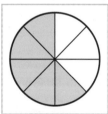	$\frac{5}{8}$ of the circle is shaded.	$\frac{3}{8}$ of the circle is shaded.	Five-eighths of the circle is shaded.

⑦
	$\frac{1}{4}$ of the square is shaded.	3 out of 4 squares are shaded.	Three-fourths of the square is shaded.

Fill in the missing fraction.

8 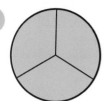 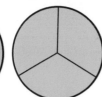  3 wholes = $\dfrac{\square}{\square}$

Shade each model to show the given fraction. Then, match the equivalent fractions.

9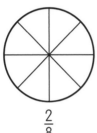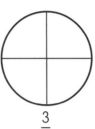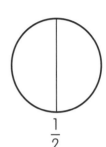

$\dfrac{2}{8}$ $\dfrac{2}{3}$ $\dfrac{3}{4}$ $\dfrac{1}{2}$

•   •   •   •

•   •   •   •

$\dfrac{2}{4}$ $\dfrac{4}{6}$ $\dfrac{1}{4}$ $\dfrac{6}{8}$

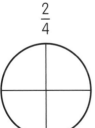  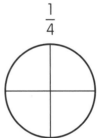 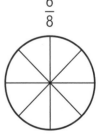

Fill in each missing fraction on the number lines.
Then, write the equivalent fractions.

10

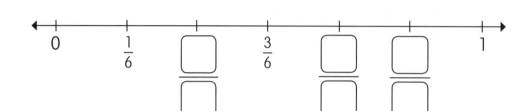

$$\frac{1}{3} = \frac{\boxed{}}{\boxed{}} \qquad \frac{\boxed{}}{3} = \frac{4}{\boxed{}}$$

11

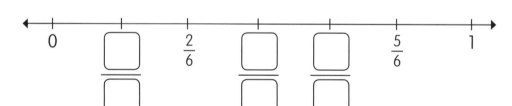

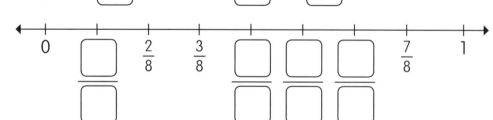

$$\frac{1}{\boxed{}} = \frac{\boxed{}}{6} = \frac{4}{\boxed{}}$$

Compare each pair of fractions. Write < or >.

12
$\frac{4}{6}$
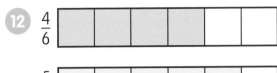
$\frac{5}{6}$

$\frac{4}{6} \bigcirc \frac{5}{6}$

13
$\frac{1}{2}$
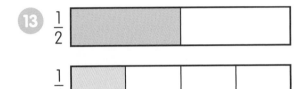
$\frac{1}{4}$

$\frac{1}{2} \bigcirc \frac{1}{4}$

14
$\frac{3}{4}$
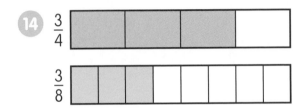
$\frac{3}{8}$

$\frac{3}{4} \bigcirc \frac{3}{8}$

Assessment Prep

Answer each question.

15 Which shape is divided equally such that each part is $\frac{1}{6}$ of the shape?

Select the **two** correct answers.

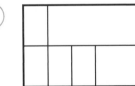

(A) (B) (C) (D)

16 Which fractions make the comparison true?

$$\frac{2}{4} > ?$$

Select the **three** correct answers.

(A) $\frac{2}{8}$ (B) $\frac{2}{3}$

(C) $\frac{2}{6}$ (D) $\frac{1}{4}$

(E) $\frac{3}{4}$

17 Which number line shows a point at $\frac{11}{8}$?

(A)

(B)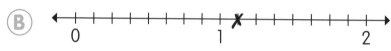

(C)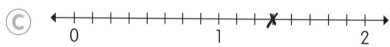

(D)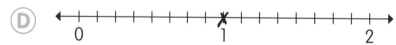

18 Look at Point X on the number line.

What fraction does X represent?

What do the denominator and the numerator of the fraction represent on the number line?

Show your answer and your explanation in the space provided.

A Lesson on Fractions

A class of 24 students was having a lesson on fractions.

1 Michelle drew a circle and divided it into equal parts.
Each part was $\frac{1}{4}$ of the circle.
Draw lines to show what her circle looked like.

2 Michelle drew another circle.
She divided it into 3 unequal parts.
Draw lines to show what her circle looked like.

© 2020 Marshall Cavendish Education Pte Ltd

3 Malik divided the shape into equal parts and colored 3 of the parts.

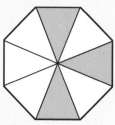

What fraction of the shape is colored?
What fraction of the shape is not colored?

4 $\frac{2}{6}$ of the students in the class wear glasses and the rest do not.
How many students in the class of 24 students wear glasses?

5 $\frac{1}{2}$ of the students in the class take the bus to school.

Use the number lines to find fractions that are equivalent to $\frac{1}{2}$.

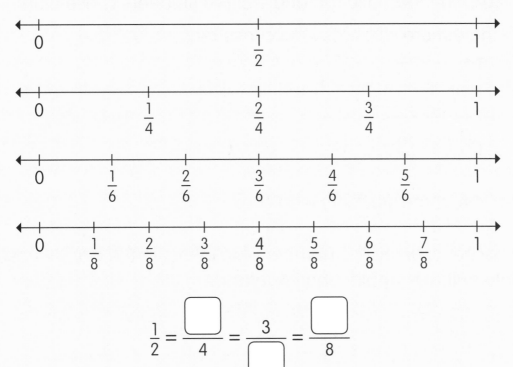

$$\frac{1}{2} = \frac{\boxed{}}{4} = \frac{3}{\boxed{}} = \frac{\boxed{}}{8}$$

6 The teacher counted the number of students in the class whose favorite color was red, blue, or yellow.

$\frac{1}{8}$ of the students chose red and $\frac{3}{8}$ of the students chose blue.

Were there more students who chose red or blue?

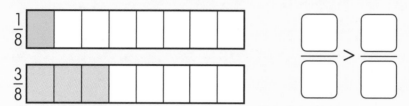

There were more students who chose _____.

7 The teacher counted the number of students in the class whose favorite fruit was apple, pear, or orange.

$\frac{2}{4}$ of the students chose apple and $\frac{2}{6}$ of the students chose pear.

Were there fewer students who chose apple or pear?

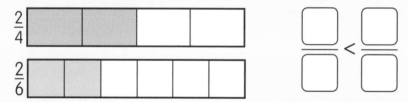

There were fewer students who chose _____.

Rubric

Point(s)	Level	My Performance
7–8	4	• Most of my answers are correct. • I showed complete understanding of what I have learned. • I used the correct strategies to solve the problems. • I explained my answers and mathematical thinking clearly and completely.
5–6.5	3	• Some of my answers are correct. • I showed some understanding of what I have learned. • I used some correct strategies to solve the problems. • I explained my answers and mathematical thinking clearly.
3–4.5	2	• A few of my answers are correct. • I showed little understanding of what I have learned. • I used a few correct strategies to solve the problems. • I explained some of my answers and mathematical thinking clearly.
0–2.5	1	• A few of my answers are correct. • I showed little or no understanding of what I have learned. • I used a few strategies to solve the problems. • I did not explain my answers and mathematical thinking clearly.

Teacher's Comments

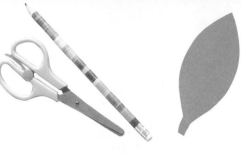

STEAM

Henri Matisse

Henri Matisse was a French painter. He also cut out colored paper to make collages. He called this kind of art "painting with scissors." Many artists like Matisse's work. They paint with scissors too.

Task

Paint with Scissors

Work in pairs.

1. Gather 8 different colors of construction paper, scissors, glue, a large sheet of paper, and a note card.

2. Cut out pieces of paper of the same shape from each construction paper. Cut 24 shapes in all.

3. Paste the cut-outs onto the large sheet of paper to make a collage.

4. Use fractions to describe your collage. Write your descriptions on the note card. Attach the note card to the bottom of the collage.

5. Show your work in a classroom art gallery. Find equivalent fractions in the art.

Chapter 8 Measurement

How heavy are the two bags?

My bag weighs 3 kilograms.

2,800 g

My bottle has 1 liter 200 milliliters of water.

My bottle has 400 milliliters of water.

Whose bottle has less water? How much less?

How can you measure mass and volume?

Name: _____   Date: _____

Measuring mass in kilograms and grams

The kilogram and gram are units of mass.
The kilogram is used to measure the mass of heavier objects.
The gram is used to measure the mass of lighter objects.

▶ **Quick Check**

Write kilograms or grams.

1. The mass of a cat is about 4 _____.

2. The mass of a nickel is about 5 _____.

Write the mass of each object.

3.

The mass of the pen is _____ grams.

4

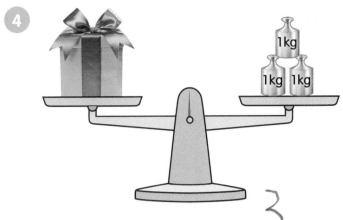

The mass of the box is ___3___ kilograms.

5

The mass of the carrots is ___6___ grams.

6

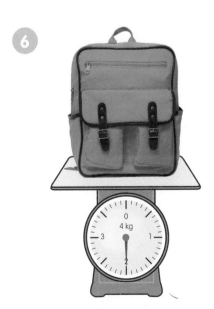

The mass of the bag is ___2___ kilograms.

Solving real-world problems about mass

There are 450 grams of flour in a bag.
Ms. Davis uses 105 grams of the flour.
How much flour is left in the bag?

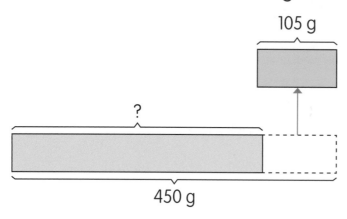

$450 - 105 = 345$

There are 345 grams of flour left in the bag.

▶ **Quick Check**

Solve. Use the bar model to help you.

7️⃣ Manuela weighs 38 kilograms.
Carlos is 7 kilograms heavier than Manuela.
How heavy is Carlos?

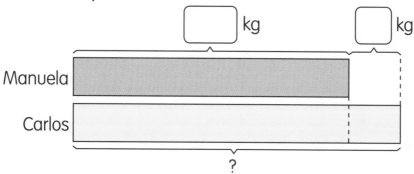

1 Mass: Kilograms and Grams

Learning Objectives:
- Estimate and find actual masses of objects by using different scales.
- Convert units of measurements between kilograms and grams.

THINK

Three bunches of carrots, A, B, and C, are placed on a
weighing scale that reads 3 kilograms 500 grams.
After Bunch C is taken off, the scale shows 2 kilograms 800 grams.
Then, Bunch B is taken off. The scale shows 1 kilogram 700 grams.
Find the mass of each bunch of carrots.

ENGAGE

What is the total mass of the pears on the two weighing scales?

LEARN Measure mass in kilograms and grams

1 The bunch of grapes has a mass of 400 grams.

The bag of flour has a mass of 1 kilogram.

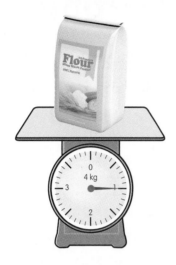

Each small marking on this scale stands for 100 grams.
100 200 300 400 500
600 700 800 900 1,000
So, 1 kilogram = 1,000 grams.

The papaya has a mass of 1 kilogram 500 grams.
What is the mass of the papaya in grams?

1 kg 500 g
— 1 kg = 1,000 g
— 500 g

1 kg 500 g = 1,000 g + 500 g
= 1,500 g

The mass of the papaya is 1,500 grams.

....

2 The mass of a bag of coffee beans is 3,600 grams.
What is its mass in kilograms and grams?

3,600 g
— 3,000 g = 3 kg
— 600 g

3,600 g = 3,000 g + 600 g
= 3 kg 600 g

Its mass is 3 kg 600 g.

© 2020 Marshall Cavendish Education Pte Ltd

Hands-on Activity Measuring mass in kilograms and grams

1. Hold a 1-kilogram weight in one hand.

2. Hold a completely filled 1-liter water bottle in the other hand.
   Compare its mass with the 1-kilogram weight.
   Fill in the blank with **more** or **less**.

   The completely filled 1-liter water bottle

   is _____ than 1 kilogram.

3. Find its actual mass using a weighing scale.

   The actual mass of the filled 1-liter water bottle

   is _____ kilogram _____ grams.

4. Repeat ① to ③ with the following objects.

Object	Compared to 1 kg	Actual Mass
Baseball bat	_____ than 1 kg	_____ kg _____ g
School bag	_____ than 1 kg	_____ kg _____ g
Note pad	_____ than 1 kg	_____ kg _____ g

Read each scale to find the mass.
Then, write each mass in grams.

2 kg 500 g = _____ g + _____ g

= _____ g

_____ kg _____ g = _____ g + _____ g

= _____ g

3

_____ kg _____ g = _____ g + _____ g

= _____ g

Read each scale to find the mass.
Then, write each mass in kilograms and grams.

4

2,400 g = _____ g + _____ g

= _____ kg _____ g

5

_____ g = _____ g + _____ g

= _____ kg _____ g

6

_____ g = _____ g + _____ g

= _____ kg _____ g

Mathematical Habit 6 Use precise mathematical language

William weighs a bag of beans.

He writes the mass in three ways.

a 1 kg 70 g

b 1,700 g

c 1,007 g

Are the masses correct? Explain.

1 kg = 1,000 g

Name: _____   Date: _____

INDEPENDENT PRACTICE

Read each scale to find the mass.
Then, write each mass in grams.

 1

_____ kg _____ g = _____ g + _____ g

= _____ g

 2

_____ kg _____ g = _____ g + _____ g

= _____ g

3

_____ kg _____ g = _____ g + _____ g

= _____ g

Read each scale to find the mass.
Then, write each mass in kilograms and grams.

4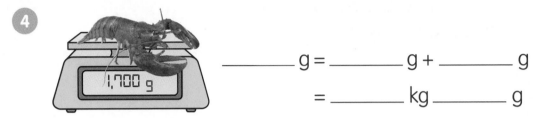

_____ g = _____ g + _____ g

= _____ kg _____ g

5

_____ g = _____ g + _____ g

= _____ kg _____ g

6

_____ g = _____ g + _____ g

= _____ kg _____ g

7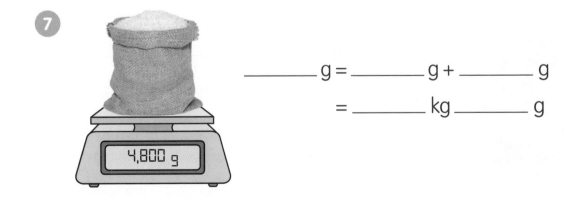

_____ g = _____ g + _____ g

= _____ kg _____ g

2 Liquid Volume: Liters and Milliliters

Learning Objectives:
- Estimate and find the volumes of liquids and capacities of containers.
- Convert units of measurements between liters and milliliters.

New Vocabulary
volume   liter (L)
milliliter (mL)   capacity

THINK

Farrah wants to measure the volume of water in a pail.
She is given a 500-milliliter water bottle and a 100-milliliter cup.
How can she find the volume of water in the pail?

ENGAGE

Some water from the jug was poured into a measuring cup.

The remaining water in the jug fills the other two measuring cups exactly.
How do you find the volume of water in the jug at first?

LEARN Measure volume in liters and milliliters

1 Each container has an amount of colored liquid in it.

The amount of liquid in a container is called the volume of the liquid.

2 This carton contains 1 liter of milk.

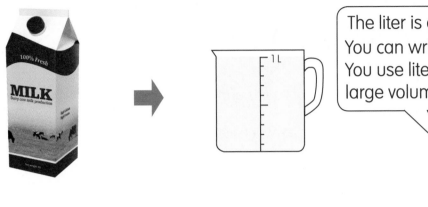

The liter is a unit of volume.
You can write **L** for liter.
You use liters to measure large volumes.

3 This syringe contains 1 milliliter of medicine.

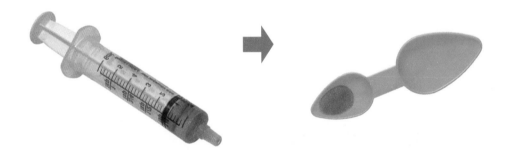

1 L = 1,000 mL

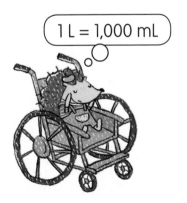

The milliliter is also a unit of volume.
You can write **mL** for milliliter.
You use milliliters to measure small volumes.

4 Each measuring cup contains some water.

Cup A

Each marking on this measuring cup stands for 100 milliliters.

Cup A contains 700 milliliters of water.

Cup B

Each marking on this measuring cup stands for 50 milliliters.

Cup B contains 400 milliliters of water.

Cup C

Each marking on this measuring cup stands for 10 milliliters.

Cup C contains 60 milliliters of water.

Hands-on Activity Measuring volume in liters and milliliters

Work in groups.

① Fill a beaker with 100 milliliters of water.

② Pour the water from the beaker into a 1-liter measuring cylinder.

③ Repeat ① and ② until the measuring cylinder is filled with water to the 1-liter mark. Count on by hundreds as you do ② .

④ How many milliliters make 1 liter?

_____ milliliters make 1 liter.

TRY Practice measuring volume in liters and milliliters

Circle each correct unit of measure.

1

A glass of juice

200 liters / milliliters

2

A cup of tea

150 liters / milliliters

3

A water cooler bottle

19 liters / milliliters

4

A pot of soup

3 liters / milliliters

Find the volume of water in each container.

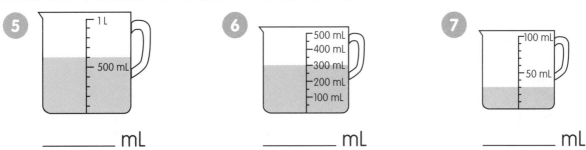

5 1 L / 500 mL

_____ mL

6 500 mL / 400 mL / 300 mL / 200 mL / 100 mL

_____ mL

7 100 mL / 50 mL

_____ mL

ENGAGE

Fill three different 🥛🥛🥛 with water to the same level.
Do they contain the same amount of water? Explain.

LEARN Measure volume and capacity

1

This bottle is partly
filled with juice.
The volume of juice
in the bottle
is 350 milliliters.

The bottle is
then completely
filled with juice.

All the juice is
poured into a
measuring cup.

> The capacity of the
> bottle is 600 milliliters.

> Capacity is the greatest amount
> of liquid a container can hold.

2   A bottle is completely filled with water.
The water is emptied into measuring cups.
Find the capacity of the bottle in milliliters.

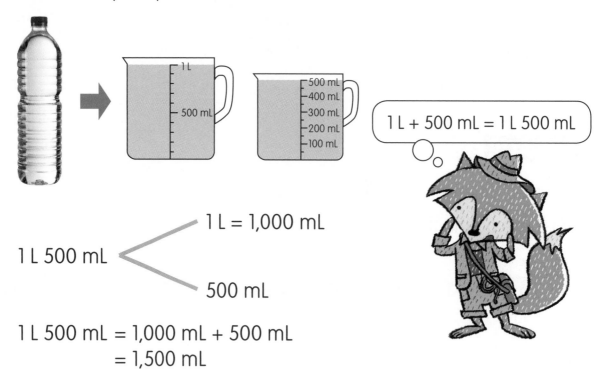

1 L 500 mL
$$\begin{cases} 1\text{ L} = 1{,}000\text{ mL} \\ \\ 500\text{ mL} \end{cases}$$

1 L + 500 mL = 1 L 500 mL

1 L 500 mL = 1,000 mL + 500 mL
         = 1,500 mL

The bottle has a capacity of 1,500 milliliters.

3   The capacity of a barrel is 8,700 milliliters.
What is its capacity in liters and milliliters?

8,700 mL
$$\begin{cases} 8{,}000\text{ mL} = 8\text{ L} \\ \\ 700\text{ mL} \end{cases}$$

8,700 mL = 8,000 mL + 700 mL
         = 8 L 700 mL

Its capacity is 8 liters 700 milliliters.

Hands-on Activity Measuring capacities of containers

Work in groups.

(1) Fill a 1-liter water bottle completely with water.

(2) Use four empty containers of different sizes.
Example:

| A | B | C | D |

(3) Compare each container with the filled 1-liter water bottle.
Estimate if the capacity of each container is more or less than 1 liter.

(4) Fill each container completely with water.
Choose a measuring tool to find the capacity of each container
in milliliters.

Math Talk

How do you know
which measuring tool
to use?

(5) Record your answers in the table below.

Container	A	B	C	D
Estimate				
Actual Capacity				

TRY Practice measuring volume and capacity

Find the total volume of liquid in each of the following.

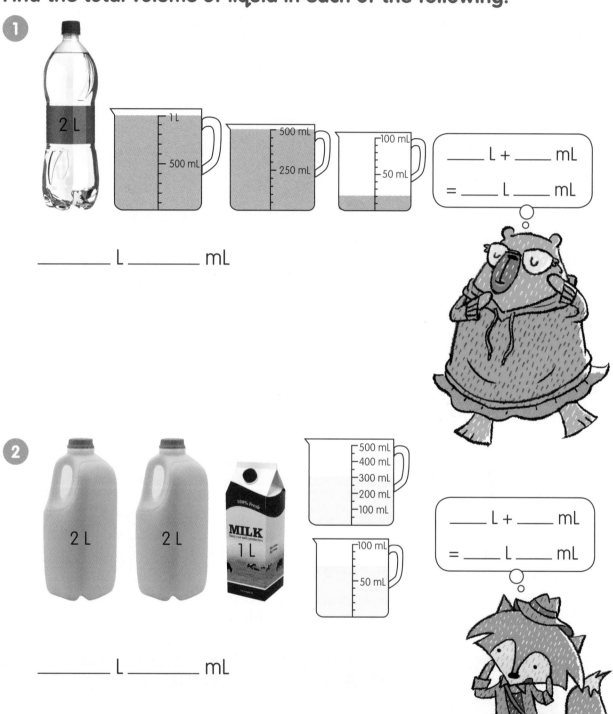

1

2 L

1 L
— 500 mL

500 mL
— 250 mL

100 mL
— 50 mL

_____ L + _____ mL

= _____ L _____ mL

_____ L _____ mL

2

2 L

2 L

MILK
100% Fresh
1 L

— 500 mL
— 400 mL
— 300 mL
— 200 mL
— 100 mL

— 100 mL
— 50 mL

_____ L + _____ mL

= _____ L _____ mL

_____ L _____ mL

Write each volume in milliliters.

3

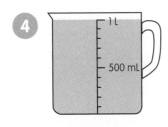   

1 L + _____ mL

= _____ L _____ mL

1 L 340 mL = _____ mL + _____ mL

= _____ mL

4

4 L + _____ mL

= _____ L _____ mL

4 L _____ mL = _____ mL + _____ mL

= _____ mL

Write each volume in liters and milliliters.

 5

This pot contains 5,600 milliliters of soup.

5,600 mL = _____ mL + _____ mL

= _____ L _____ mL

 6

This bowl contains 3,200 milliliters of water.

3,200 mL = _____ mL + _____ mL

= _____ L _____ mL

 7

This tin contains 4,900 milliliters of paint.

4,900 mL = _____ mL + _____ mL

= _____ L _____ mL

Name: _____ Date: _____

INDEPENDENT PRACTICE

Estimate the capacity of each of the following.
Write more or less in each blank.

1 The capacity of a bathtub is _____ than 1 liter.

2 The capacity of a drinking glass is _____ than 1 liter.

3 The capacity of an ice bucket is _____ than 1 liter.

4 The capacity of a tablespoon is _____ than 1 liter.

Estimate the capacity of each of the following.
Write liters or milliliters in each blank.

5 The capacity of a pail is 3 _____.

6 The capacity of a mug is 250 _____.

7 The capacity of a water bottle is 500 _____.

8 The capacity of a fish tank is 10 _____.

Find the volume of liquid in each container.
Then, write each volume in milliliters.

9

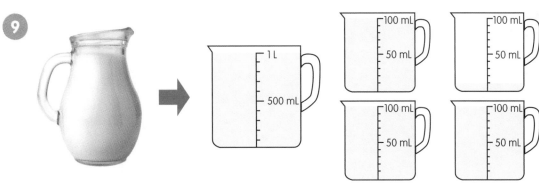

_____ L _____ mL = _____ mL + _____ mL

= _____ mL

10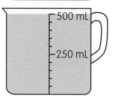

_____ L _____ mL = _____ mL + _____ mL

= _____ mL

Write the capacity of each container in liters and milliliters.

11  The capacity of this bucket is 4,500 milliliters.

4,500 mL = _____ mL + _____ mL

= _____ L _____ mL

12  The capacity of this flask is 2,800 milliliters.

2,800 mL = _____ mL + _____ mL

= _____ L _____ mL

Name: _____ Date: _____

3 Real-World Problems: One-Step Problems

Learning Objective:
• Use bar models to solve one-step real-world problems involving measurement.

**THINK**

The mass of three apples and an orange is 1 kilogram 300 grams.
The mass of an apple and the orange is 700 grams.
If all the apples have the same mass, find the mass of an apple.

ENGAGE

Draw a number bond to show 1 kilogram 200 grams.
How can you subtract 500 grams from 1 kilogram 200 grams using the number bond?

 Solve one-step real-world problems involving measurement

1 The total mass of a watermelon and a can of beans
   is 3 kilograms 700 grams.
   The mass of the can of beans is 500 grams.
   What is the mass of the watermelon in grams?

 Understand the problem.

> How heavy are the two items?
> How heavy is the can of beans?
> What do I need to find?

STEP 2 Think of a plan.
I can draw a bar model.

STEP 3 Carry out the plan.

3 kg 700 g

?   500 g

3 kg 700 g = 3 kg + 700 g
           = 3,000 g + 700 g
           = 3,700 g

3,700 − 500 = 3,200

The mass of the watermelon is 3,200 grams.

> 3 kg 700 g < 3 kg
> 700 g

STEP 4 Check the answer.
I can work backwards to check my answer.

> 3,200 + 500 = 3,700
> 3,700 g = 3 kg 700 g
> My answer is correct.

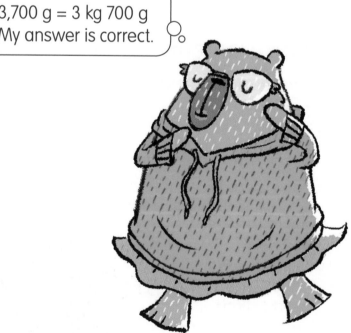

2 Mr. Carter pours some milk equally into 3 bottles.
There are 650 milliliters of milk in each bottle.
Find the total volume of milk in the 3 bottles in
liters and milliliters.

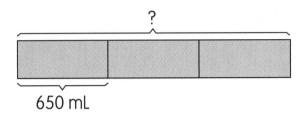

650 mL

$650 \times 3 = 1,950$

$1,950 \text{ mL} = 1,000 \text{ mL} + 950 \text{ mL}$
$\quad\quad\quad\quad = 1 \text{ L } 950 \text{ mL}$

The total volume of milk in the 3 bottles is 1 liter 950 milliliters.

3 There are 24 liters of water in a barrel.
Ricardo pours all the water equally into 4 tanks.
How much water is there in each tank?
Give your answer in milliliters.

24 L

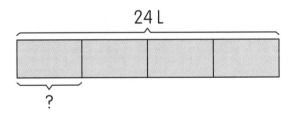

?

$24 \div 4 = 6$

$6 \text{ L} = 6,000 \text{ mL}$

There are 6,000 milliliters of water in each tank.

TRY Practice solving one-step real-world problems involving measurement

Solve. Use the bar model to help you.

1. The mass of Box A is 2 kilograms.
   The mass of Box B is 980 grams.
   How much heavier is Box A than Box B?
   Give your answer in grams.

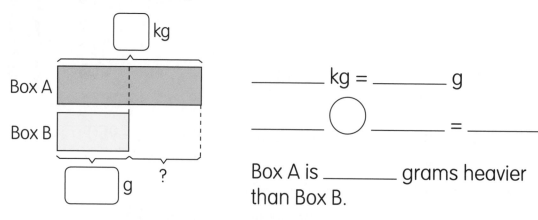

_____ kg = _____ g

_____ $\bigcirc$ _____ = _____

Box A is _____ grams heavier than Box B.

2. Ms. Hill made 650 milliliters of orange juice on Monday.
   She made 1,750 milliliters of orange juice on Tuesday.
   How much orange juice did she make on both days?
   Give your answer in liters and milliliters.

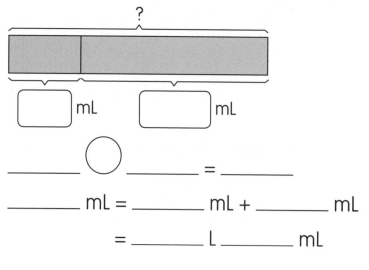

_____ $\bigcirc$ _____ = _____

_____ mL = _____ mL + _____ mL

= _____ L _____ mL

She made _____ liters _____ milliliters
of orange juice on both days.

Solve. Draw a bar model to help you.

3 Mario buys 50 kilograms of flour for his bakery.
He repacks the flour equally into 10 bags.
How much flour is there in each bag?
Give your answer in grams.

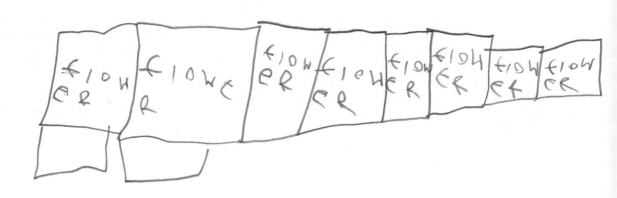

4 A chef poured 9 cups of water into a pot.
Each cup contained 240 milliliters of water.
How much water did the chef pour into the pot?
Give your answer in liters and milliliters.

MEMORY GAME!

What you need:

Players: 3 to 5
Materials: Cards of measurement

What to do:

1 Shuffle the cards and arrange them face down on the table.

2 Player 1 flips two cards over and sees if the measurements are equal. If they are equal, he or she gets to keep the pair of cards. Player 1 gets another turn.

3 If the measurements are not equal, flip the cards back. The game moves on to the next player until there are no more cards left.

Who is the winner?

The player with the most cards wins.

INDEPENDENT PRACTICE

Solve. Use the bar model to help you.

1. The mass of a bag of seeds is 2 kilograms 500 grams.
   It is 900 grams lighter than a basket of fruit.
   Find the mass of the basket of fruit.
   Give your answer in grams.

   [ ] kg [ ] g   [ ] g

   bag of seeds

   basket of fruit

   ?

2 Chef Ali has 3,400 grams of blueberries.
   He uses 700 grams of the blueberries for a pie.
   Find the mass of blueberries Chef Ali has left.
   Give your answer in kilograms and grams.

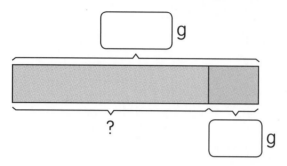

Solve. Draw a bar model to help you.

3 There are 8,000 milliliters of water in a tank.
   Justin pours all the water equally into 4 pails.
   How many liters of water are there in each pail?

4 The mass of Parcel A is 800 grams.
The mass of Parcel B is twice the mass of Parcel A.
What is the mass of Parcel B?
Give your answer in kilograms and grams.

5 The capacity of a cup is 230 milliliters.
The capacity of a bottle is 4 times the capacity of the cup.
What is the total capacity of the cup and the bottle?
Give your answer in liters and milliliters.

Mathematical Habit 6 Use precise mathematical language

Write a real-world problem using the information below.

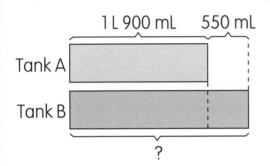

1 L 900 mL = 1,000 mL + 900 mL
            = 1,900 mL

1,900 + 550 = 2,450

Tank B contains 2,450 milliliters of water.

_____

_____

_____

_____

_____

Problem Solving with Heuristics

1 **Mathematical Habit** **2** **Use mathematical reasoning**
Find the mass of each item.

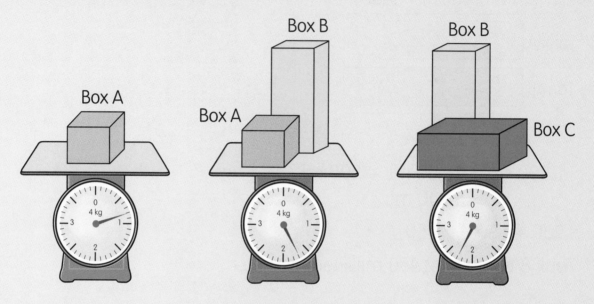

a   What is the mass of Box A?

b   What is the mass of Box B?

c   What is the mass of Box C?

2 **Mathematical Habit 6** Use precise mathematical language

Show how these two bottles can be used to measure 200 milliliters of water exactly.
Write the steps needed to solve the problem.

Bottle A   Bottle B

CHAPTER WRAP-UP

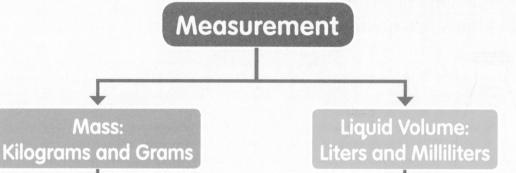

Measurement

Mass: Kilograms and Grams

You can convert measurements of mass between kilograms (kg) and grams (g).

1 kg = 1,000 g

2 kg 500 g = 2,000 g + 500 g
= 2,500 g

3,600 g

3,600 g = 3,000 g + 600 g
= 3 kg 600 g

Liquid Volume: Liters and Milliliters

Volume is the amount of liquid in a container.
Capacity is the greatest amount of liquid a container can hold.

You can convert measurements of volume between liters (L) and milliliters (mL).

1 L = 1,000 mL

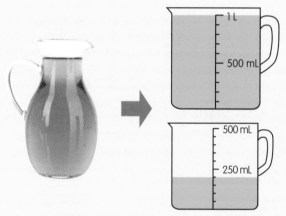

1 L 200 mL = 1,000 mL + 200 mL
= 1,200 mL

The kettle has a capacity of 2,100 milliliters.

2,100 mL = 2,000 mL + 100 mL
= 2 L 100 mL

Name: _____ Date: _____

Find the mass of each item.

1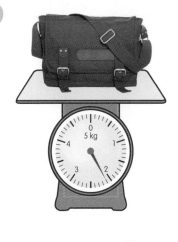

_____ g

2

_____ kg _____ g

Estimate the capacity of each of the following.
Write more or less in each blank.

3 The capacity of a teaspoon is _____ than 1 liter.

4 The capacity of a barrel is _____ than 1 liter.

5 The capacity of a soup bowl is _____ than 1 liter.

6 The capacity of a swimming pool is _____ than 1 liter.

Find the volume of liquid in the bottle.

7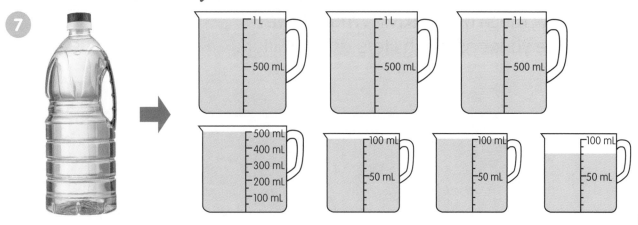

There are _____ milliliters of oil in the bottle.

Write the capacity in liters and milliliters.

(8)

The capacity of this kettle is 1,800 milliliters.

1,800 mL = _____ L _____ mL

Solve. Draw a bar model to help you.

(9) Valery's bag weighs 2,700 grams.
Brianna's bag weighs 3,100 grams.
What is the total mass of their bags?
Give your answer in kilograms and grams.

(10) Mr. Wright has 9 bottles of oil.
Each bottle contains 590 milliliters of oil.
How much oil does Mr. Wright have?
Give your answer in liters and milliliters.

11 The capacity of a bucket is 3 liters.
1,230 milliliters of water are poured into the bucket.
How much water is needed to fill the bucket completely?
Give your answer in milliliters.

Assessment Prep

Answer each question.

12 Kaitlyn pours 2 liters 500 milliliters of water into a measuring cup.
Which marking shows the correct amount of water?

Ⓐ Marking P

Ⓑ Marking Q

Ⓒ Marking R

Ⓓ Marking S

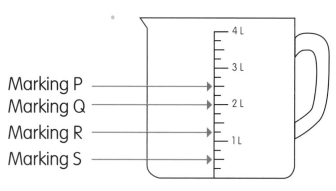

13 A pot contains 2 liters 650 milliliters of soup.
How many milliliters of soup does the pot contain?
Enter your answer in the space provided.

14 There are 6 kilograms 200 grams of rice in a container.
Ms. Reyes uses 900 grams of the rice.
How many grams of rice are left in the container?
Enter your answer in the space provided.

Name: _____   Date: _____

A Science Project

Charles is doing a project about measuring mass and volume.

1 He needs to find the total mass of two bags.
What is the total mass of the bags in grams?

2 Charles needs to use 5 wooden blocks for his project.
Each block weighs 700 grams.
What is the total mass of the blocks?
Give your answer in kilograms and grams.

© 2020 Marshall Cavendish Education Pte Ltd

3 A tank contains some water.
Charles pours all the water into the measuring cups below.
How many milliliters of water are there in all?

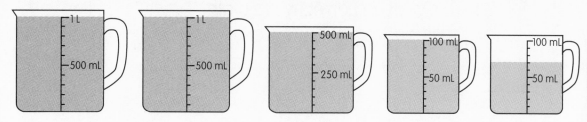

4 Charles has to choose a beaker.
The beaker needs to hold at least 1 liter of water.
Charles decides to use Beaker C.
Has Charles chosen correctly? Explain.

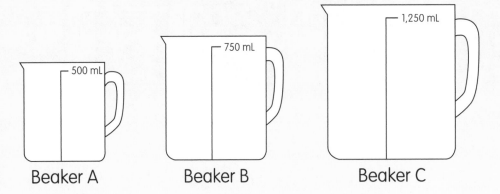

Beaker A   Beaker B   Beaker C

Rubric

Point(s)	Level	My Performance
7–8	4	• Most of my answers are correct. • I showed complete understanding of what I have learned. • I used the correct strategies to solve the problems. • I explained my answers and mathematical thinking clearly and completely.
5–6.5	3	• Some of my answers are correct. • I showed some understanding of what I have learned. • I used some correct strategies to solve the problems. • I explained my answers and mathematical thinking clearly.
3–4.5	2	• A few of my answers are correct. • I showed little understanding of what I have learned. • I used a few correct strategies to solve the problems. • I explained some of my answers and mathematical thinking clearly.
0–2.5	1	• A few of my answers are correct. • I showed little or no understanding of what I have learned. • I used a few strategies to solve the problems. • I did not explain my answers and mathematical thinking clearly.

Teacher's Comment

STEAM

Life Aboard the International Space Station

Astronauts from around the world live and work on the International Space Station. They are busy while living in space. They walk in space. They do experiments. They keep the station in good shape. They plan and present programs to schools. They post news online. Other than work, they also spend time having fun.

Task

An Astronaut for a Day

Work in pairs.

1. Go to the library to learn more about the life of an astronaut on the space station. Visit NASA online to read, listen, and watch videos about the life of astronauts.

2. Imagine being an astronaut on the space station. Your day begins at 6 A.M. How do you spend the next 12 hours?

3. On a large sheet of paper, draw the different things you do.

4. Draw a timeline for the 12 hours. Color and label the timeline to show how much time you spend on each activity.

5. Make a bar graph to show the data.

Chapter 9
Area and Perimeter

What is the relationship between area and perimeter?

Name: _____ Date: _____

Multiplying using an area model

$7 \times 7 = ?$

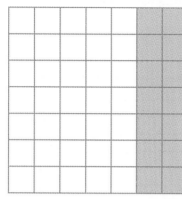

$7 \times 7 = 5$ groups of $7 + 2$ groups of 7
$\qquad = (5 \times 7) + (2 \times 7)$
$\qquad = 35 + 14$
$\qquad = 49$

▶ **Quick Check**

Find each missing number.
Use the area model to help you.

① $6 \times 8 = ?$

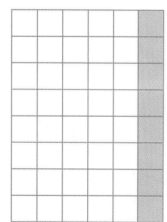

$6 \times 8 = 5$ groups of $8 +$ _____ group of 8

$\qquad = (5 \times 8) + ($ _____ $\times 8)$

$\qquad =$ _____ $+$ _____

$\qquad =$ _____

Showing a shape on dot paper and grid paper

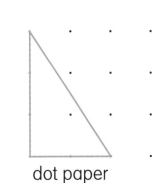

dot paper

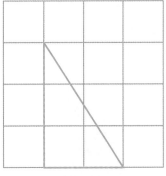

grid paper

▶ Quick Check

Copy each shape on the dot paper or grid paper.

2

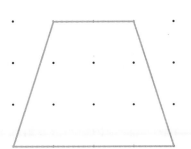

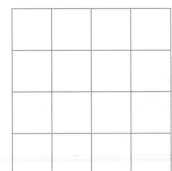

3

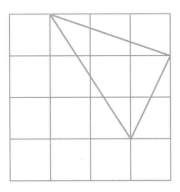

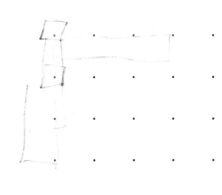

Measuring length using metric units

Meters (m) and centimeters (cm) are metric units of length.
Meters are used to measure longer lengths.

Joseph jumped 1 meter.

Centimeters are used to measure shorter lengths.

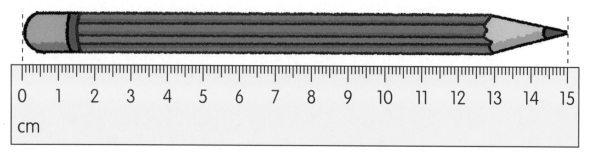

The pencil is 15 centimeters long.

▶ **Quick Check**

Circle the correct unit for each length.

4️⃣ A classroom is 5 meters / centimeters long.

5️⃣ A spoon is 10 meters / centimeters long.

6️⃣ A parcel is 24 meters / centimeters tall.

7️⃣ A streetlamp is 3 meters / centimeters tall.

Measuring length using customary units

Both feet (ft) and inches (in.) are customary units of length.
Feet are used to measure longer lengths.
Inches are used to measure shorter lengths.

1 foot (ft) = 12 inches (in.)

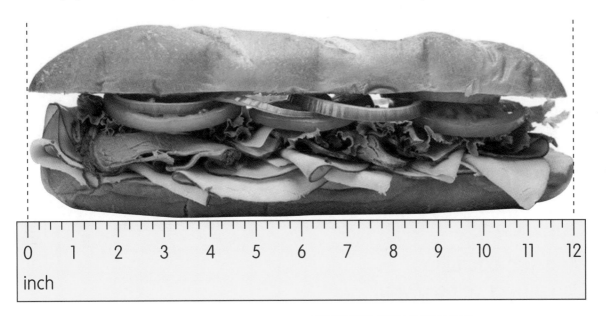

This ruler is smaller than in real life.

▶ **Quick Check**

Circle the correct unit for each length.

8 A table is 3 feet / inches tall.

9 A paper clip is 1 foot / inch long.

10 A notebook is 5 feet / inches tall.

11 A floor mat is 2 feet / inches long.

Measuring lengths with a ruler

This line is 5 centimeters long.

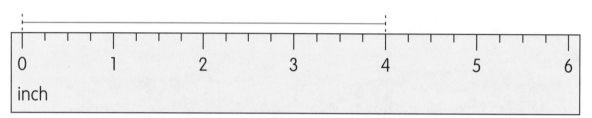

This line is 4 inches long.

▶ **Quick Check**

Measure each line.
Use a ruler to help you.

12 _____

_____ centimeters

13 _____

_____ inches

14 _____

_____ inches

15 _____

_____ centimeters

1 Area

Learning Objectives:
- Understand the meaning of area.
- Use square units to find area of plane figures made of squares and half-squares.
- Compare the area of plane figures and make plane figures of the same area.

New Vocabulary
square unit
area

THINK

Compare the area of your tabletop with your teacher's.
How do you know which is larger?

ENGAGE

Use 5  to create as many different figures as you can.

Sketch each figure. How many figures did you create?
Share your figures with your partner.

LEARN Use square units to find area

1 Look at the figures.

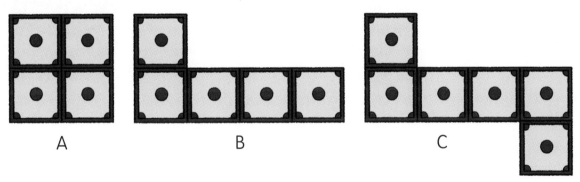

A   B   C

Count the number of square tiles in each figure.

Figure A is made up of 4 square tiles.
Figure B is made up of 5 square tiles.
Figure C is made up of 6 square tiles.

Let each square tile stand for 1 square unit.

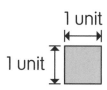

1 unit

1 unit

Figure A is made up of 4 square tiles.
So, its area is 4 square units.

Figure A has an area of 4 square units.
Figure B has an area of 5 square units.
Figure C has an area of 6 square units.

Area is the number of square tiles needed to cover the surface of each figure. It is measured in square units.

Hands-on Activity Using square units to find area

(1) Use 4 square tiles to make as many different figures. Draw them below.

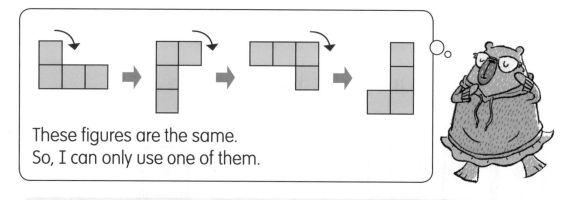

These figures are the same.
So, I can only use one of them.

(2) What is the area of each figure?

The area of each figure is _____ square units.

TRY Practice using square units to find area

Look at each figure and answer each question.

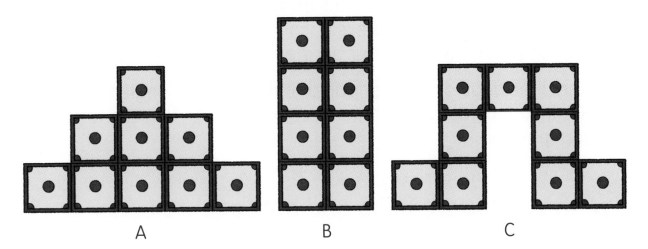

A   B   C

1 How many square tiles make each figure?

a   Figure A is made up of _____ square tiles.

b   Figure B is made up of _____ square tiles.

c   Figure C is made up of _____ square tiles.

2 Each square tile is 1 square unit.
What is the area of each figure?

a   The area of Figure A is _____ square units.

b   The area of Figure B is _____ square units.

c   The area of Figure C is _____ square units.

3 Which figure has the smallest area?

Figure _____ has the smallest area.

4 Which two figures have the same area?

Figures _____ and _____ have the same area.

ENGAGE

1 Use a square piece of paper to make two triangles.
Are they of the same size? How do you know?
What fraction of the square is each triangle?
Explain your thinking to your partner.

2 Use a rectangular piece of paper to make two triangles.
Are the triangles of the same size? Explain your thinking to
your partner.

LEARN Use square units and half-square units to find area

1 Figure A is made up of squares and half-squares.

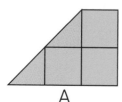

◻ is 1 square unit.

◺ is $\frac{1}{2}$ square unit.

◺ ◺ is equal to ◨.

◺ ◺ make 1 square unit.

Figure A is made up of 4 squares of
the same size. Its area is 4 square units.

Math Talk

Matías drew a circle on a square grid.
He thinks the area of the circle is about
13 square units. Is he correct?
Why do you think so?

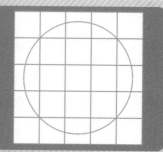

© 2020 Marshall Cavendish Education Pte Ltd

Work in pairs.

Activity 1   Using square units and half-square units to find area

1. Use four square tiles and two half-square tiles
   to make four different figures.
   Draw them below.

Check if your figures
are the same.

2. What is the area of each figure?

   The area of each figure is _____ square units.

Activity 2   Estimating the area of a figure drawn on a square grid

1 Place a leaf on the square grid.
Trace the outline of the leaf.

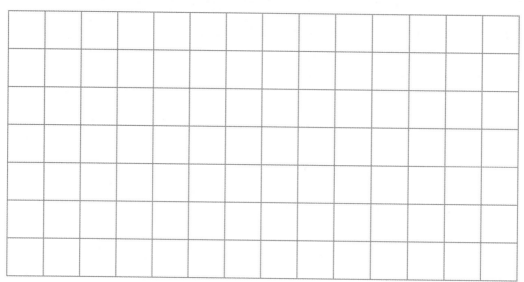

2 Count the squares to estimate the area of the leaf.

Count 1 square unit.

Count $\frac{1}{2}$ square unit.

Count 1 square unit.

Count 0 square units.

The area of the leaf is about _____ square units.

3 **Mathematical Habit 6** Use precise mathematical language
How did you find the area?

Draw two different figures with the same area on the grid. Use squares (■) or half-squares (◣) in each figure.

12

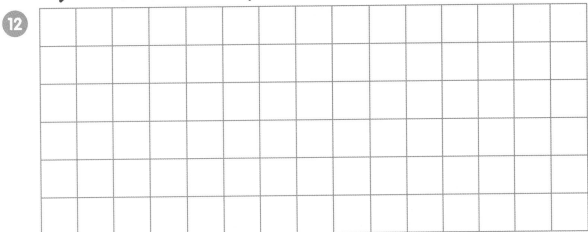

Add squares (■) or half-squares (◣) to each figure to make its area 7 square units.

13

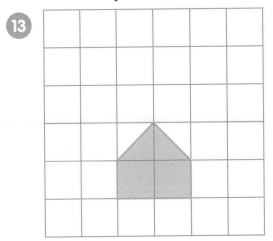

14

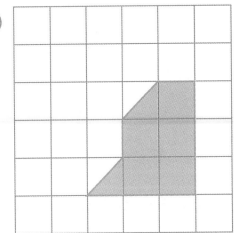

Cut out each triangle tile below.
Use all the tiles to make three figures with different areas.
Paste each figure in the space below.
Then, fill in each blank.

15

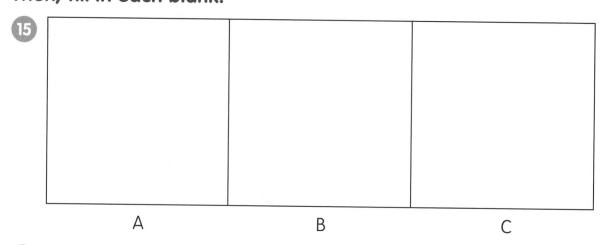

A   B   C

16 Which figure has the smallest area?

Figure _____ has the smallest area.

17 Which figure has the largest area?

Figure _____ has the largest area.

18 Order the figures from the largest to the smallest area.

_____   _____   _____
  largest   smallest

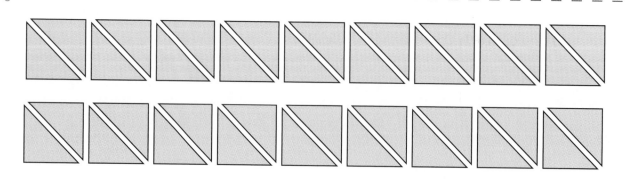

Square Units (cm² and in²)

Learning Objective:
- Use square centimeters and square inches to find and compare the area of plane figures.

New Vocabulary
square centimeter (cm²)
square inch (in²)

THINK

Use 10 square tiles to form different figures.
Make sure the sum of all the sides in each figure is different.
Which of your figures has the greatest sum of all the sides?

ENGAGE

1 Use a 1-centimeter square grid to show how you can use four small squares to make one larger square. What is the area of the new square?

2 Use a 2-centimeter square grid to build a larger square. What would be the area of the new square?

LEARN Find area in square centimeters

1 This is a 1-centimeter square.
Each side of the square is 1 centimeter long.
Its area is 1 square centimeter.
It is written as 1 cm².

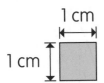

The square centimeter (cm²) is a metric unit of measure for area.

A 2-centimeter square is made up of four 1-centimeter squares. Its area is 4 square centimeters (cm²).

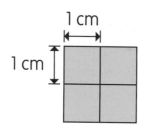

A 3-centimeter square is made up of nine 1-centimeter squares. Its area is 9 square centimeters (cm²).

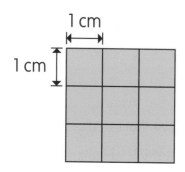

Count the number of 1-centimeter squares.

2 The figure is made up of 1-centimeter squares and half-squares.

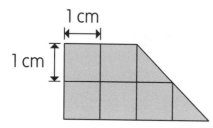

The figure is made up of five 1-centimeter squares and 2 half-squares.

The area of the figure is 6 square centimeters.

ENGAGE

Draw a square with sides measuring 3 inches.
How many 1-inch squares do you need to make the square you drew?
Compare your drawing with your partner's.

LEARN Find area in square inches

1. This is a 1-inch square.
Each side of the square is 1 inch long.
Its area is 1 square inch.
It is written as 1 in^2.

1 in.

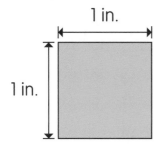

1 in.

The square inch (in^2) is a customary unit of measure for area.

A 2-inch square is made up of four 1-inch squares.
Its area is 4 square inches (in^2).

1 in.

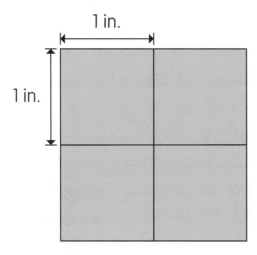

1 in.

A 3-inch square is made up of nine 1-inch squares.
Its area is 9 square inches (in^2).

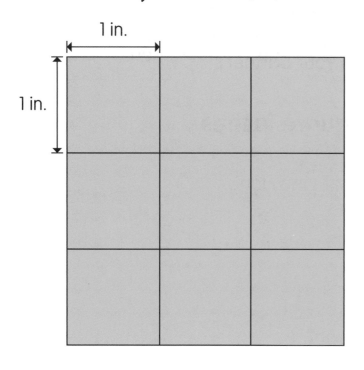

Count the number of 1-inch squares.

2 The figure is made up of 1-inch squares and half-squares.

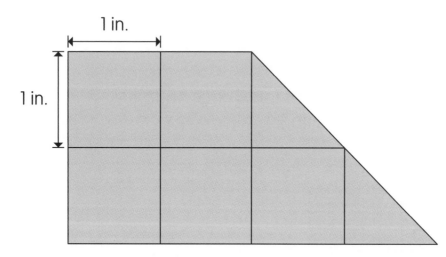

The area of the figure is 6 square inches.

The figure is made up of five 1-inch squares and two half-squares.

© 2020 Marshall Cavendish Education Pte Ltd

Name: _____   Date: _____

3 Square Units (m² and ft²)

Learning Objective:
• Use square meters and square feet to find and compare the area of plane figures.

 THINK

Hana wants to lay square tiles on the floor of her rectangular room.
She measures the room in square meters.
However, the store only sells tiles in square feet.
What should Hana do to buy the correct number of tiles?

ENGAGE

What is the area of a square with sides of

a 1 meter,   **b** 2 meters,   **c** 3 meters,   **d** 4 meters?

Draw a sketch of each square and label its area.
What pattern do you notice?

LEARN Find area in square meters

1. Each side of this tabletop is 1 meter long.
   The area of the tabletop is 1 square meter.
   It is written as 1 m².

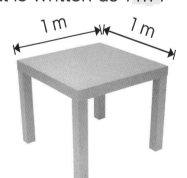

1 m   1 m

Which do you think is larger,
1 square centimeter or
1 square meter? Why?

The square meter (m²) is also a metric unit of measure for area.
1 square meter (m²) is larger than 1 square centimeter (cm²).

The area of the tabletop is 1 square meter.
The sticker has an area of 1 square centimeter.

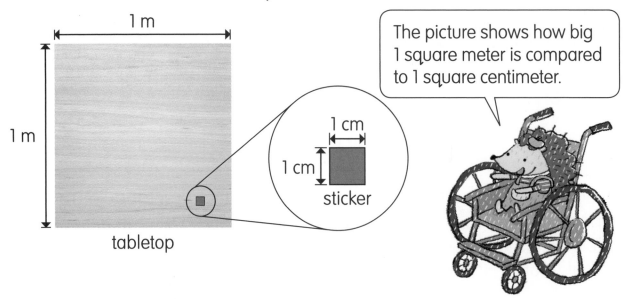

tabletop

The picture shows how big 1 square meter is compared to 1 square centimeter.

A 4-meter square is made up of 16 1-meter squares.
The area of each 1-meter square is 1 square meter.
So, the area of the 4-meter square is 16 square meters (m^2).

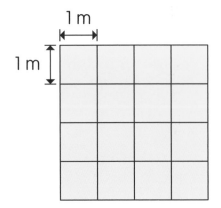

Count the number of 1-meter squares.

Mathematical Habit 3 Construct viable arguments

Peyton and Luis are asked to find the area of the figure below.

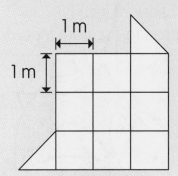

1 m

1 m

Peyton thinks the answer is 10 square meters.
Luis thinks the answer is 11 square meters.
Who is correct? Why?

ENGAGE

A classroom floor is laid using square tiles.
The area of each square tile is 1 square foot.
How do you find the area of the classroom floor?

LEARN Find area in square feet

1 Each side of this floor tile is 1 foot long.
The area of the floor tile is 1 square foot.
It is written as 1 ft².

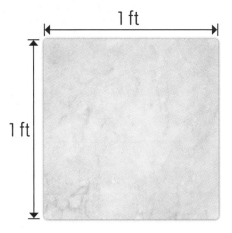

1 ft

1 ft

Which do you think is
larger, 1 square inch or
1 square foot? Why?

The square foot (ft²) is also a customary unit of measure for area.
1 square foot (ft²) is larger than 1 square inch (in²).

The area of the floor tile is 1 square foot.
The stamp has an area of 1 square inch.

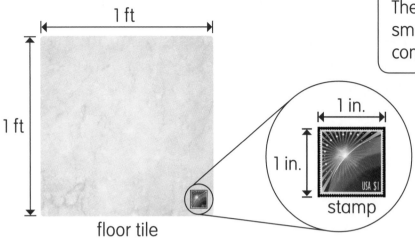

floor tile

stamp

The picture shows how small 1 square inch is compared to 1 square foot.

A 5-feet square is made up of 25 1-foot squares.
The area of each 1-foot square is 1 square foot.
So, the area of the 5-feet square is 25 square feet (ft^2).

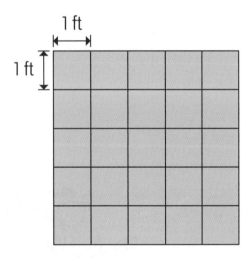

Count the number of 1-foot squares.

① Use gift wrap and tape to make two square pieces of paper. The first piece should have an area of 1 square meter and the other 1 square foot.

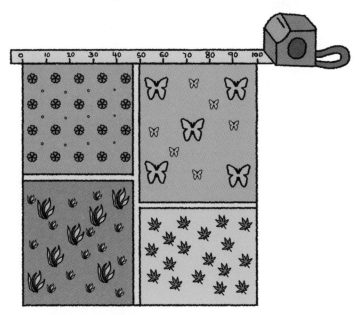

1 square meter   1 square foot

② Use both pieces of paper to estimate the area of these objects in your classroom.

Object	Estimated Area	
	Square Meters (m²)	Square Feet (ft²)
a Door		
b Your table		
c Whiteboard		

TRY Practice finding area in square feet

Find the area of each figure.
Then, answer each question below.
Each figure is not drawn to scale.

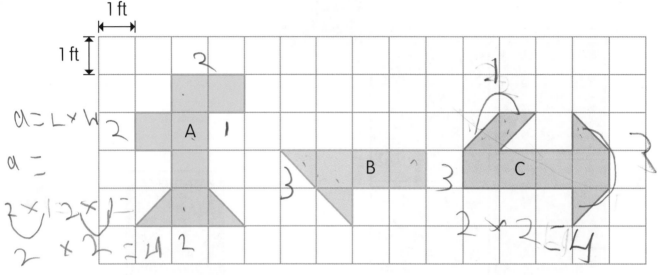

1 ft

1 ft

handwritten: a = L × W   a =   2 × 1 2 × 1 =   2 × 2 = 4

2   A 1   2   B   3   3   1   C   2   2 × 2 = 4

1. The area of Figure A is **4** square feet.   *handwritten:* 3 × 3 = 6

2. The area of Figure B is **6** square feet.

3. The area of Figure C is **4** square feet.

4. Which figure has the smallest area? *B*

   Figure **B**

5. Which figure has the largest area?

   Figure **A an a B**

6. Which figure has an area that is 2 square feet larger than Figure B?
   A

   Figure **A**

Find the area of each figure in the correct square units.
Then, fill in the table below.
Each figure is not drawn to scale.

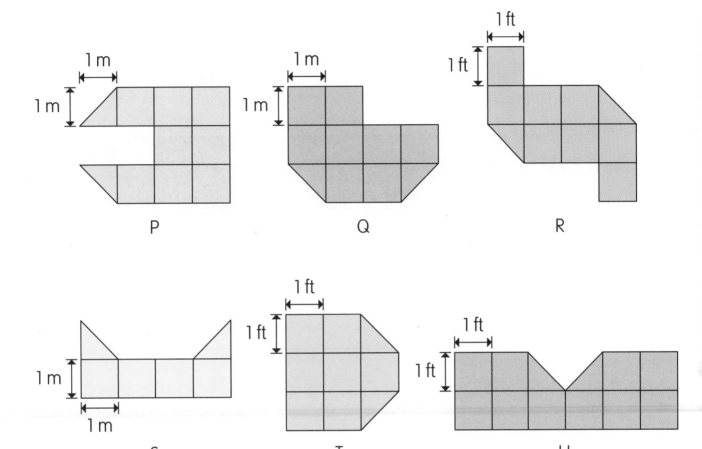

P

Q

R

S

T

U

	Figure	Area
8	P	
9	Q	
10	R	
11	S	
12	T	
13	U	

**Make square pieces of paper with an area
of 1 square meter and 1 square foot.
Then, estimate the area of each object using the squares.**

14. The area of my kitchen floor is about _____ square meters.

15. The area of my bed is about _____ square feet.

Object	Estimated Area	
	Square Meters (m²)	Square Feet (ft²)
16. Dining tabletop		
17. Pillowcase		
18. Cupboard door		
19. Television screen		
20. Bedroom floor		

Name: _____ Date: _____

4 Perimeter and Area

Learning Objectives:
- Understand the meaning of perimeter.
- Find the perimeter of plane figures formed using small squares.
- Compare the areas and perimeters of two plane figures.
- Find the area of rectangles using multiplication and addition.

New Vocabulary
perimeter

THINK

Tomas has four square tiles. Each square tile is 2 centimeters long. How many figures can he form using all four tiles without overlapping? What do you notice about the perimeters and areas of the figures?

ENGAGE

Find the area of the figure. Then, find the length of the rubber band that forms the figure. What other ways can you use to find the answers? Share your ideas with your partner.

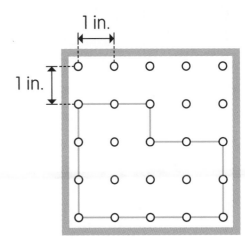

LEARN Find the area and perimeter of a figure

1 Jane used a piece of rope to make the figure below.

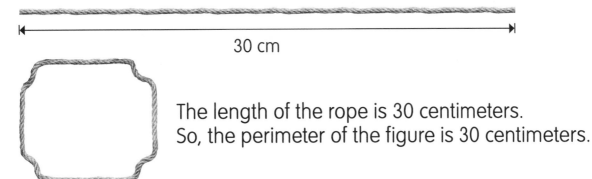

30 cm

The length of the rope is 30 centimeters.
So, the perimeter of the figure is 30 centimeters.

The perimeter of a figure is the total length around it.

2 Look at the rectangle.

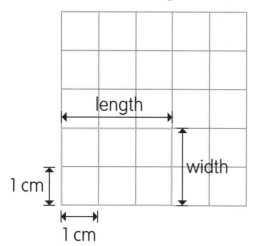

Count the number of squares inside the rectangle.
The area of the rectangle is 6 square centimeters.

Add the length of each side of the rectangle to find its perimeter.
3 + 2 + 3 + 2 = 10
So, the perimeter of the rectangle is 10 centimeters.

3 Look at the figure.

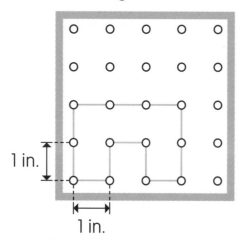

These inch squares are smaller than in real life.

The area of this figure is 5 square inches.
Its perimeter is 12 inches.

Perimeter can be measured in centimeters (cm), inches (in.), meters (m), and feet (ft).

Area can be measured in square centimeters (cm^2), square inches (in^2), square meters (m^2), and square feet (ft^2).

4 Look at the figures below.

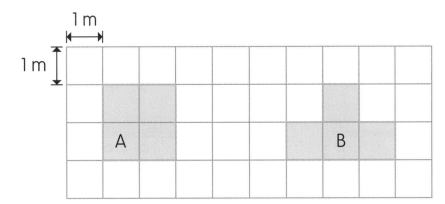

Area = 4 m²
Perimeter = 8 m

Area = 4 m²
Perimeter = 10 m

Figure A and Figure B have the same area. Do they have the same perimeter?

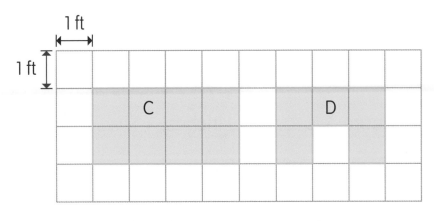

Area = 8 ft²
Perimeter = 12 ft

Area = 5 ft²
Perimeter = 12 ft

Do Figure C and Figure D have the same area? What do you notice about their perimeters?

Hands-on Activity — Finding the area and perimeter of a figure

Work in pairs.

1. Use a 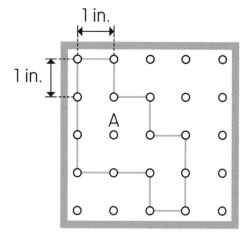 and a rubber band to make each figure below.

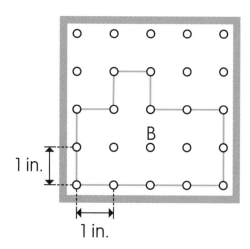

2. Count to find the perimeter and area of each figure.

The area of Figure A is _____ square inches.

The perimeter of Figure A is _____ inches.

The area of Figure B is _____ square inches.

The perimeter of Figure B is _____ inches.

3. What do you notice about the areas and perimeters of the figures?

© 2020 Marshall Cavendish Education Pte Ltd

TRY Practice finding the area and perimeter of a figure

Find the area and perimeter of each figure.
Then, answer each question below.
Each figure is not drawn to scale.

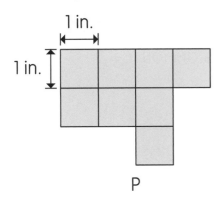

P

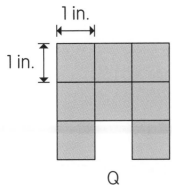

Q

1. The area of Figure P is _____ square inches.

2. The perimeter of Figure P is _____ inches.

3. The area of Figure Q is _____ square inches.

4. The perimeter of Figure Q is _____ inches.

5. Do Figures P and Q have the same area?
   Explain your answer.

   _____

   _____

6. Do Figures P and Q have the same perimeter?
   Explain your answer.

   _____

   _____

ENGAGE

Your teacher will provide you with some unit squares.
Arrange them into quadrilaterals in different ways.
Find the area of each shape formed using multiplication.

LEARN Find the area of a rectangle using multiplication

① Angelia's quilt is made up of 1-foot squares of cloth.
What is the area of her quilt?

▶ **Method 1**

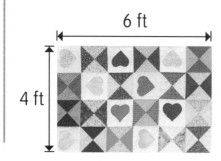

6 ft

4 ft

Multiply the side lengths of the rectangle.

$6 \times 4 = 24$

The area of her quilt is 24 square feet.

▶ **Method 2**

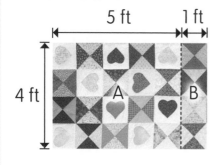

5 ft   1 ft

4 ft   A   B

STEP 1 Separate the figure into two rectangles.

STEP 2 Multiply to find the area of each rectangle.

Area of Rectangle A = 5×4
= 20 ft^2

Area of Rectangle B = 1×4
= 4 ft^2

STEP 3 Add the two areas together.
$20 + 4 = 24$

The area of her quilt is 24 square feet.

TRY Practice finding the area of a rectangle using multiplication

Fill in each missing number. Then, find the area of each figure. Each figure is not drawn to scale.

1.

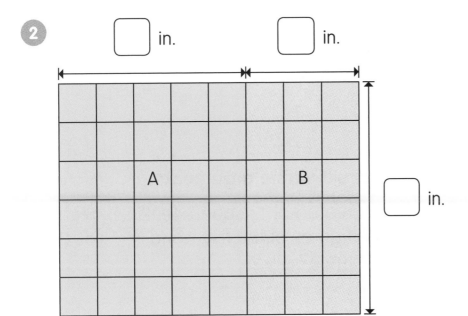

☐ units

☐ units

Length = _____ units

Width = _____ units

Area = _____ × _____

= _____ square units

2. ☐ in.   ☐ in.

☐ in.

Area of Rectangle A = _____ × _____

= _____ in²

Area of Rectangle B = _____ × _____

= _____ in²

Area of figure = _____ + _____

= _____ in²

The area of the figure is _____ square inches.

Find the area of each rectangle.
Each rectangle is not drawn to scale.

3

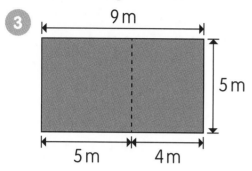

9 m

5 m

5 m   4 m

Area = _____ m²

4

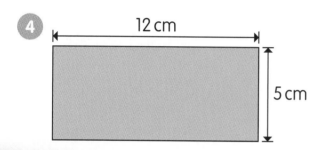

12 cm

5 cm

Area = _____ cm²

Mathematical Habit 3 Construct viable arguments

A rectangular fish pond has an area of 12 square feet.
Brooklyn drew some possible figures of the fish pond.
Which of the figures are not correct?
Explain your answer.

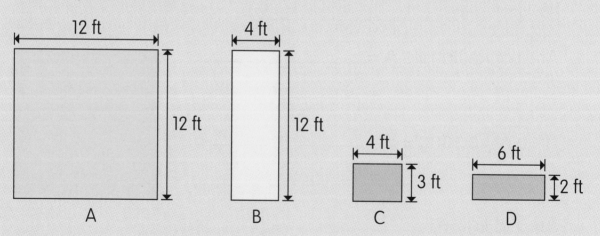

12 ft

12 ft

A

4 ft

12 ft

B

4 ft

3 ft

C

6 ft

2 ft

D

© 2020 Marshall Cavendish Education Pte Ltd

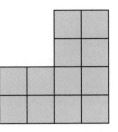

ENGAGE

This figure can be made up of rectangle(s) and square(s). Show different ways to form the shape using rectangle(s) and square(s). Share your ideas with your partner.

LEARN Find the area of a figure by separating it into rectangles

1 Look at the figure below.

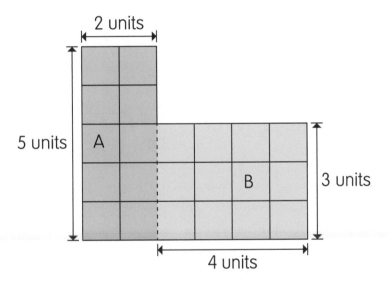

The figure can be separated into two rectangles.
To find the area of the figure, add the areas of each rectangle.
You can use multiplication to find the area of each rectangle.

Area of Rectangle A = 5 × 2
         = 10 square units

Area of Rectangle B = 4 × 3
         = 12 square units

Area of the figure = 10 + 12
        = 22 square units

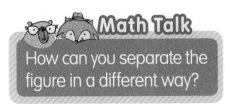

Math Talk

How can you separate the figure in a different way?

The area of the figure is 22 square units.

© 2020 Marshall Cavendish Education Pte Ltd

TRY Practice finding the area of a figure by separating it into rectangles

Divide each figure into rectangles.

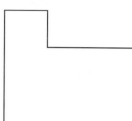

2

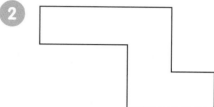

Find the area of each figure.
Each figure is not drawn to scale.

3 A school has an "L" shaped swimming pool. What is the area of the swimming pool?

Area of Rectangle A = _____ ◯ _____

= _____ m²

Area of Rectangle B = _____ ◯ _____

= _____ m²

Area of the swimming pool = _____ ◯ _____

= _____ m²

The area of the swimming pool is _____ square meters.

4 The figure shows the shape of a piece of cardboard.
What is the area of the piece of cardboard?

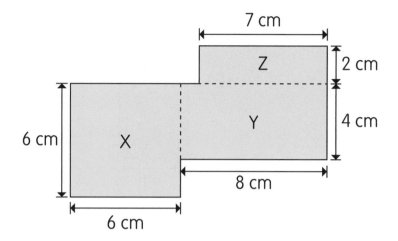

Area of Square X = _____ ◯ _____

= _____ cm²

Area of Rectangle Y = _____ ◯ _____

= _____ cm²

Area of Rectangle Z = _____ ◯ _____

= _____ cm²

Area of the piece of cardboard

= _____ ◯ _____ ◯ _____

= _____ cm²

The area of the piece of cardboard is _____ square centimeters.

5 The figure shows the shape of Melanie's backyard.
What is the area of her backyard?

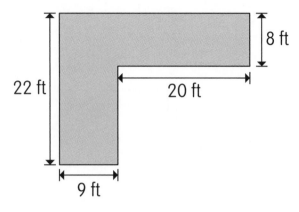

6 Tristan cuts a piece of paper in the figure shown below.
What is the area of the figure?

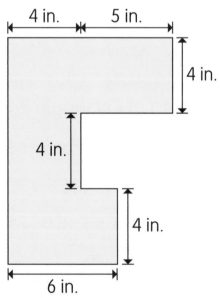

Name: _____ Date: _____

INDEPENDENT PRACTICE

Find the area and perimeter of each figure.
Each figure is not drawn to scale.

1

1 cm

1 cm

A

Area = _____ cm²

Perimeter = _____ cm

2

1 in.

1 in.

B

Area = _____ in²

Perimeter = _____ in.

3

1 m

1 m

C

Area = _____ m²

Perimeter = _____ m

4

1 ft

1 ft

D

Area = _____ ft²

Perimeter = _____ ft

**Find the area and perimeter of each figure in the correct units.
Then, answer each question.
Each figure is not drawn to scale.**

5

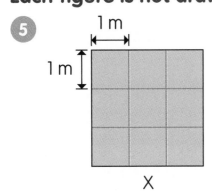

Area = _____

Perimeter = _____

6

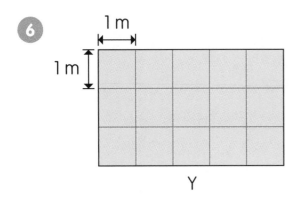

Area = _____

Perimeter = _____

7 Do Figures X and Y have the same area? _____

8 Do Figures X and Y have the same perimeter? _____

9 What is the difference between the area and perimeter of a figure?
Explain.

_____

_____

_____

_____

_____

Use square tiles to draw two different figures.
Each figure should have an area of 5 square centimeters.

10
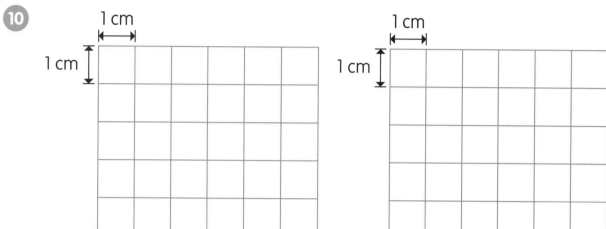

11 What do you notice about the perimeters of the figures drawn?

_____

_____

Use the grid to draw two different figures.
Each figure should have a perimeter of 8 centimeters.

12
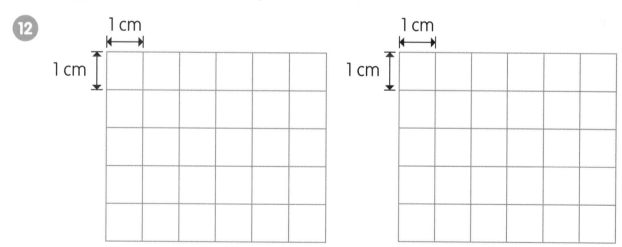

13 What do you notice about the areas of the figures drawn?

_____

_____

Divide each rectangle into two smaller rectangles.
Then, fill in each missing number to find the area.

14

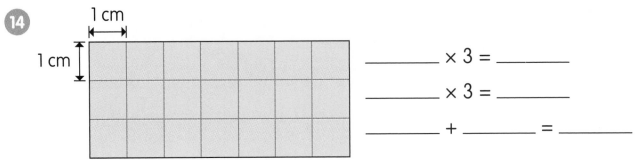

1 cm

1 cm

_____ × 3 = _____

_____ × 3 = _____

_____ + _____ = _____

The area of the rectangle is _____ square centimeters.

15

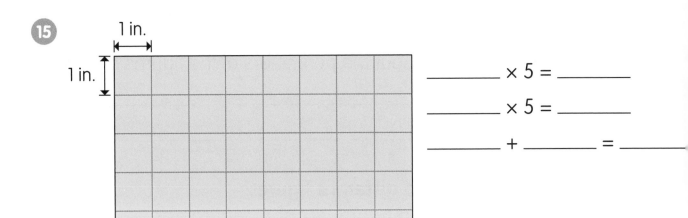

1 in.

1 in.

_____ × 5 = _____

_____ × 5 = _____

_____ + _____ = _____

The area of the rectangle is _____ square inches.

Multiply to find the area of the rectangle.

16

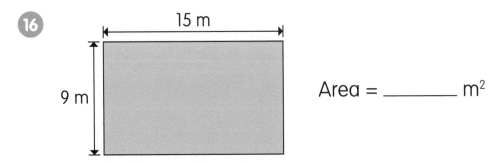

15 m

9 m

Area = _____ m²

Draw lines to separate each figure into rectangles.
Then, find the area of each figure.
Each figure is not drawn to scale.

17

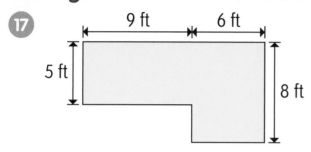

18

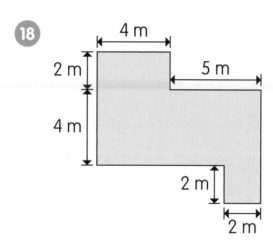

**The Flores family drew two designs for their new pool.
Find the area of each pool design and answer the question.
Each figure is not drawn to scale.**

19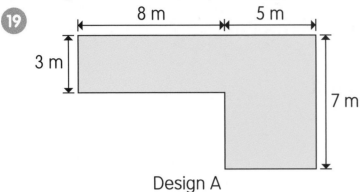

Design A

20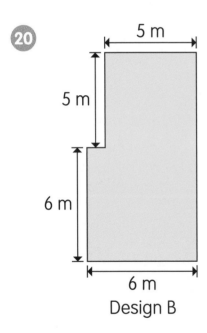

Design B

21 The Flores family wants to build the pool using the design with a larger area. Which design should they pick?

Design _____

5 More Perimeter

Learning Objectives:
- Find the perimeter of a plane figure by adding its sides.
- Choose the appropriate tools and units of length to measure perimeter.
- Solve problems involving perimeter.

THINK

Aidan used a rubber band to make a rectangle on a geoboard.
The rectangle had a length of 8 inches and a width of 4 inches.
Aidan stretched the length of the rectangle without increasing its width.
If the area of the rectangle doubled, what is the new perimeter of
the rectangle?

ENGAGE

Use a 4-centimeter piece of string to form a square.
What is the length of each side?
How can you find the perimeter of the square?

LEARN Find the perimeter of a figure

1 What is the perimeter of the figure?

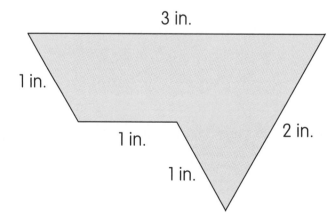

3 in.

1 in.

1 in.

1 in.

2 in.

Perimeter of figure
= 3 + 2 + 1 + 1 + 1
= 8 in.

The perimeter of the figure
is 8 inches.

2 Each side of the square is 6 centimeters long.
Find its perimeter.

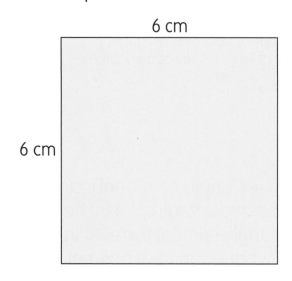

6 cm

6 cm

How many sides
does a square have?

Perimeter = 6 + 6 + 6 + 6
= 24 cm

Its perimeter is 24 centimeters.

Hands-on Activity **Finding the perimeter of a figure**

1 The sticks below are of different lengths.
Use some of the following sticks to form a figure.

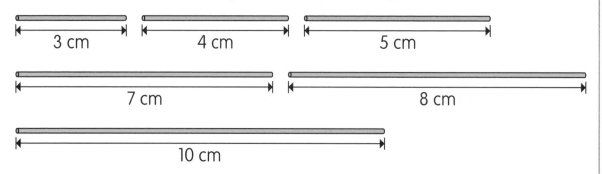

3 cm

4 cm

5 cm

7 cm

8 cm

10 cm

Example:

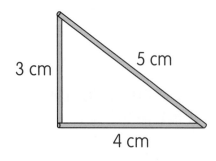

3 cm

5 cm

4 cm

② Draw the figure in the space below.

③ What is the perimeter of the figure?

The perimeter of the figure is _____ centimeters.

④ Repeat ① to ③ by forming another figure.

The perimeter of the figure is _____ centimeters.

TRY Practice finding the perimeter of a figure

Find the perimeter of the figure.
The figure is not drawn to scale.

1

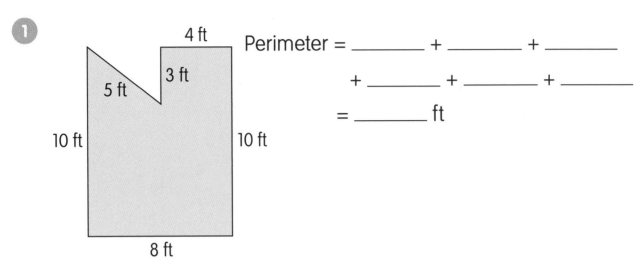

Perimeter = _____ + _____ + _____

\qquad\qquad + _____ + _____ + _____

\qquad\qquad = _____ ft

Use a centimeter ruler or inch ruler to measure the sides
of each figure. Then, find the perimeter of each figure.

2

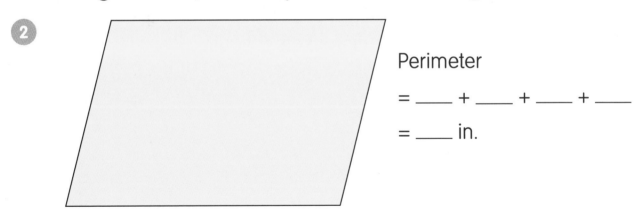

Perimeter

= ___ + ___ + ___ + ___

= ___ in.

3

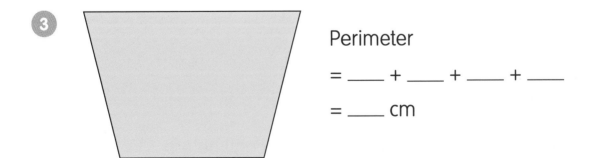

Perimeter

= ___ + ___ + ___ + ___

= ___ cm

Find the perimeter of each figure.
Each figure is not drawn to scale.

4

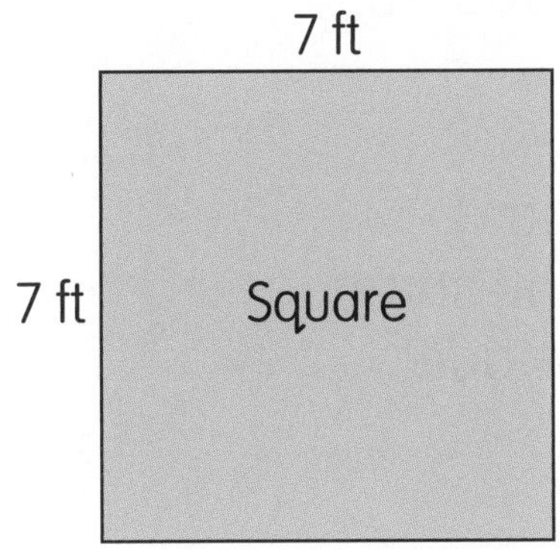

7 ft

7 ft   Square

Perimeter = _____ ft

5

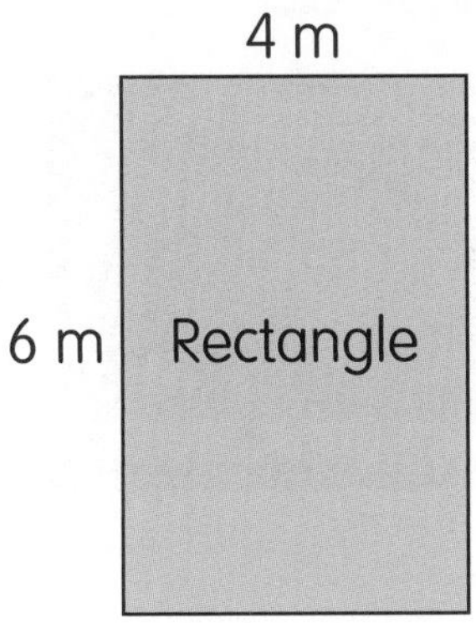

4 m

6 m   Rectangle

Perimeter = _____ m

Solve.

6 Each side of a square is 8 meters long.
Find the perimeter of the square.

The perimeter of the square is _____ meters.

ENGAGE

1 Make a square of sides 8 units on a geoboard.
What is the area of the square?

2 Make different rectangles on the geoboard.
Keep the perimeters of the rectangles the same.
Record the area of each rectangle you made.
What pattern do you see?

LEARN Solve problems involving perimeter

1 The width of a rug is 12 feet.
Its length is twice its width.
What is the perimeter of the rug?

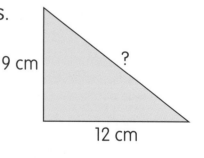

12 ft

?

Length = 2 × 12
          = 24 ft

Perimeter = 24 + 12 + 24 + 12
              = 72 ft

The perimeter of the rug is 72 feet.

2 The perimeter of a triangle is 36 centimeters.
Find the unknown length of the triangle.

9 cm   ?

12 cm

12 + 9 + ? = 36

Unknown length = 36 − 12 − 9
                    = 15 cm

The unknown length of the triangle is 15 centimeters.

TRY Practice solving problems involving perimeter

Solve.
Each figure is not drawn to scale.

1　Oliver uses nine square tiles to form a large square.
Each square tile is 5 inches long.
What is the perimeter of the large square?

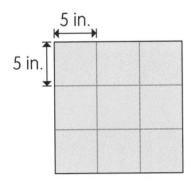

Side length of large square

= 3 × _____

= _____ in.

Perimeter of large square

= _____ + _____ + _____ + _____

= _____ in.

The perimeter of the large square is _____ inches.

What is another way to find the perimeter of the large square?

2 The length of a rectangular piece of paper is twice its width.

    a   If the width of the piece of paper is 6 centimeters, find its perimeter.

    b   If the length of the piece of paper is 6 centimeters, find its area.

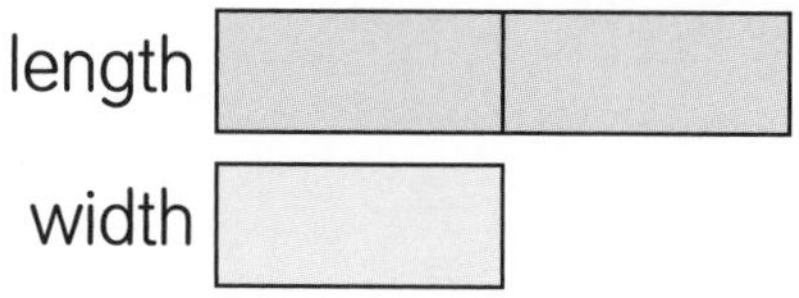

length

width

3 The figure shows the shape of a garden. The garden has a perimeter of 50 meters. What is the unknown length?

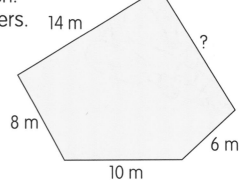

Unknown length

= 50 – ____ – ____ – ____ – ____

= ____ m

The unknown length is ____ meters.

4 A 30-centimeter piece of string was used to form a rectangle. The length of the rectangle was 10 centimeters. Find the width of the rectangle.

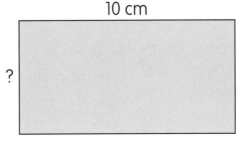

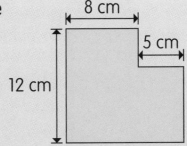

Mathematical Habit 2 Use mathematical reasoning

Kwan found the perimeter of the figure given only the information shown. The figure is not drawn to scale. Explain how he did it.

Use a ▨ and a rubber band for each of the following.

1. Make as many figures as you can with a perimeter of 8 units. What do you notice about their areas?

2. Make as many figures as you can with a perimeter of 12 units. What do you notice about their areas?

3. Make a square with sides of 4 units each. What do you notice about the perimeter and the area of the square?

4. Make as many different rectangles as you can with an area of 12 square units. How many different rectangles can you make?

INDEPENDENT PRACTICE

**Find the perimeter of each figure in the correct unit.
Each figure is not drawn to scale.**

1

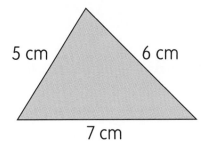

5 cm   6 cm

7 cm

Perimeter = _____

2

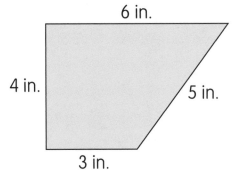

6 in.

4 in.   5 in.

3 in.

Perimeter = _____

3

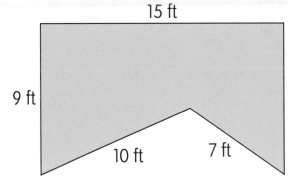

15 ft

9 ft   9 ft

10 ft   7 ft

Perimeter = _____

4

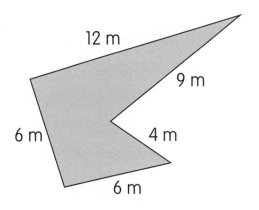

12 m

9 m

6 m   4 m

6 m

Perimeter = _____

Use a centimeter ruler or inch ruler to measure the sides of each figure. Then, find the perimeter of each figure.

Perimeter = _____ in.

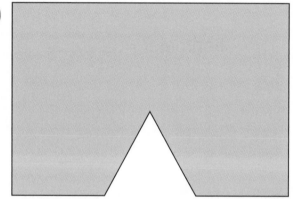

Perimeter = _____ in.

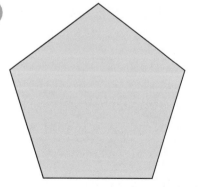

Perimeter = _____ cm

**Find the perimeter of each figure in the correct unit.
Each figure is not drawn to scale.**

8

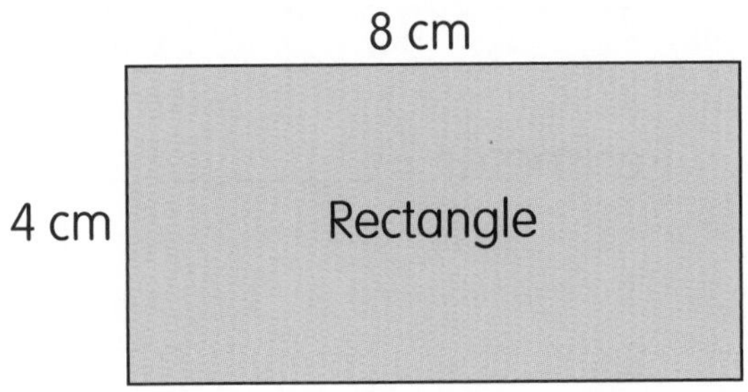

8 cm

4 cm | Rectangle

Perimeter = _____

9

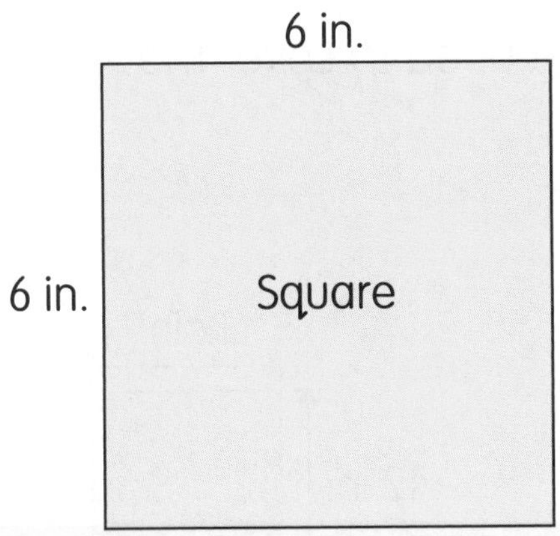

6 in.

6 in. | Square

Perimeter = _____

10

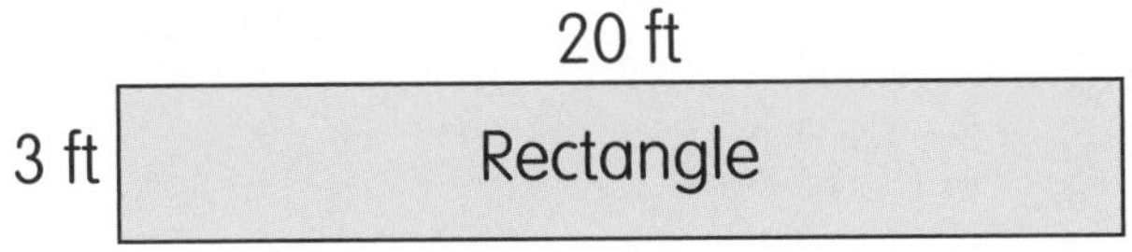

20 ft

3 ft | Rectangle

Perimeter = _____

11

8 m

Square

Perimeter = _____

Use the figure to solve each question.
Each figure is not drawn to scale.

12 Four square tiles with 12-inch sides are used to cover the surface of a large square.
Find the perimeter of the large square.

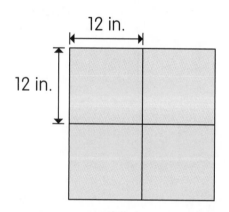

12 in.

12 in.

13 Kaylee took a walk along the edge of a rectangular field once. How far did she walk?

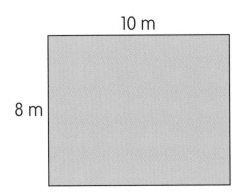
10 m

8 m

14 Jayden wants to decorate a rectangular card by pasting ribbon around. What is the length of ribbon he needs?

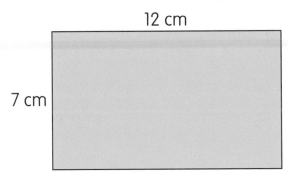
12 cm

7 cm

15 The length of a rectangular hall is 3 times its width.
The perimeter of the hall is 32 meters.
Find the length and width of the hall.

16 Sophia has two square cardboard pieces.
Each side is 6 inches long.
She places them side by side to form a rectangle.
What is the perimeter of the rectangle?

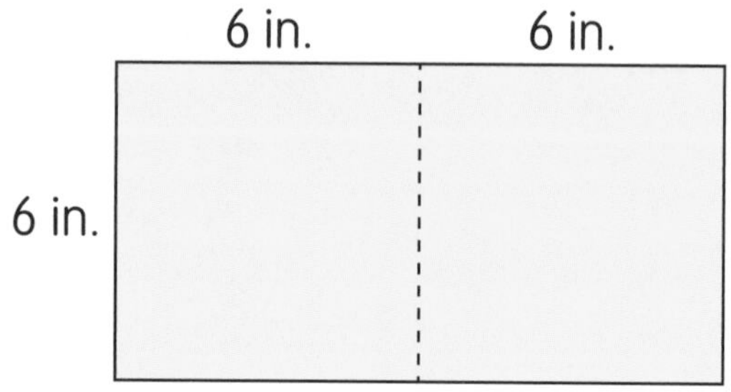

6 in.	6 in.

6 in.

17 Four square tables are arranged next to one another to form a large rectangular table.
The perimeter of the large rectangular table is 30 feet.
What is the perimeter of each square table?

18 The triangle has a perimeter of 25 inches.
What is the unknown length of the triangle?

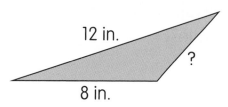

12 in.

?

8 in.

19 Manuel has a rectangular card that has a perimeter
of 96 centimeters. The width of the card is 18 centimeters.
What is the length of the card?

?

18 cm

Name: _____ Date: _____

Mathematical Habit 3 Construct viable arguments

Colton wrote his answers for the perimeter of the squares and rectangles in the table.

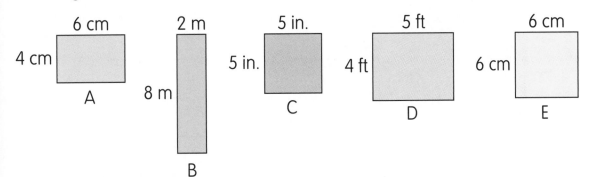

Figure	Length	Width	Perimeter
A	6 cm	4 cm	(10 cm)
B	8 m	2 m	(20 cm)
C	5 in.	5 in.	(20 in^2)
D	5 ft	4 ft	18 ft
E	(6 m)	(6 m)	(36 m)

His mistakes are circled in red. Explain his mistakes.

_____

_____

_____

_____

_____

_____

Problem Solving with Heuristics

1 **Mathematical Habit 8** **Look for patterns**

Look at the pattern below.

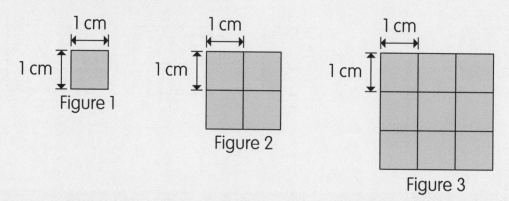

a   How many 1-centimeter squares are there in each figure?

Figure	Number of Squares
1	1
2	1 + _____ = _____
3	1 + _____ + _____ = _____

b   What pattern do you notice?

c   How many 1-centimeter squares will there be in Figure 10?

2 | **Mathematical Habit 2** | Use mathematical reasoning

Jasmín wants to build a pen for her pet rabbit.
She has 36 feet of fencing to build a rectangular pen in her yard.
Help her plan the length and width of the pen.

a Fill in the table with all the possible ways Jasmín can build the pen with a perimeter of 36 feet.

Length	Width	Perimeter
1 ft	17 ft	36 ft

b What are some concerns that Jasmín needs to think of when planning for the pen?

? What is the relationship between area and perimeter?

Area and Perimeter

Area

Area is the amount of space covered. It is measured in square units like square centimeters (cm^2), square inches (in^2), square meters (m^2), and square feet (ft^2).

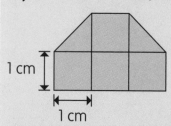

The figure is made up of four squares and two half-squares.
Its area is 5 square centimeters.

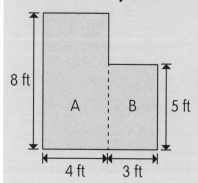

Area of Rectangle A = 8 × 4
                    = 32 ft^2
Area of Rectangle B = 5 × 3
                    = 15 ft^2
Area of figure = 32 + 15
               = 47 ft^2

The area of the figure is 47 square feet.

Perimeter

The perimeter of a figure is the total length around it. It is measured in units of length like centimeters (cm), inches (in.), meters (m), and feet (ft).

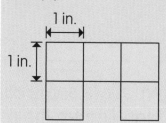

The perimeter of the figure is 12 inches.

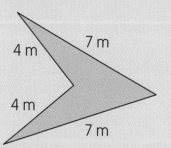

Perimeter = 4 + 7 + 7 + 4
          = 22 m

The perimeter of the figure is 22 meters.

Name: _____ Date: _____

Find the area of each figure.

 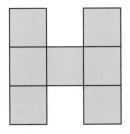

Area = _____ square units

 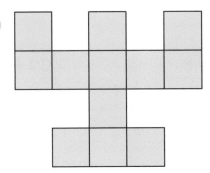

Area = _____ square units

 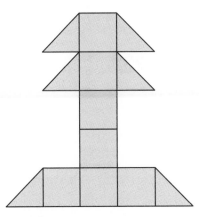

Area = _____ square units

 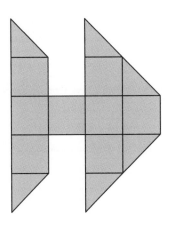

Area = _____ square units

Find the area of each figure in square centimeters (cm².)
Then, answer each question.
Each figure is not drawn to scale.

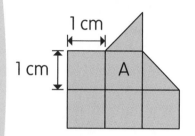

5

Figure	A	B	C
Area	_____ cm²	_____ cm²	_____ cm²

6 Which figure has the largest area?   Figure _____

7 Which figure has the smallest area?   Figure _____

Find the area of each figure in square inches (in².)
Then, answer the question below.
Each figure is not drawn to scale.

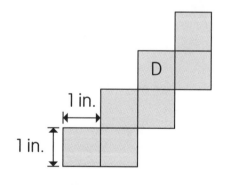
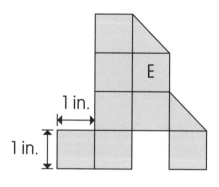
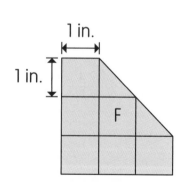

8

Figure	D	E	F
Area	_____ in²	_____ in²	_____ in²

9 Which figures have the same area?

Figures _____ and _____

Find the area of each figure in square meters (m²).
Then, order the figures according to their sizes.
Each figure is not drawn to scale.

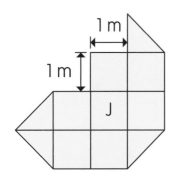

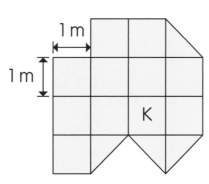

10

Figure	J	K	L
Area	_____ m²	_____ m²	_____ m²

11 Ordered from largest to smallest:

_____ _____ _____
largest   smallest

Find the area of each figure in square feet (ft²).
Then, make an X on the figure that has a different area.
Each figure is not drawn to scale.

12
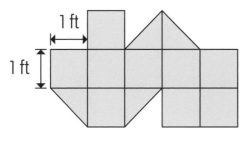
Area = _____ ft²

13
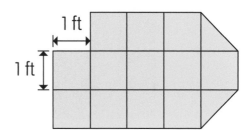
Area = _____ ft²

14
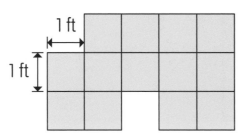
Area = _____ ft²

15
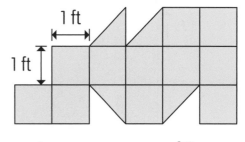
Area = _____ ft²

Use the grid to draw two different figures.
Each figure should have an area of 12 square centimeters.
Then, find the perimeter of each figure.

16

1 cm

1 cm

1 cm

1 cm

Perimeter = _____ cm   Perimeter = _____ cm

Divide each figure into two smaller rectangles.
Then, find the area of each figure by adding
the areas of the two rectangles.

17

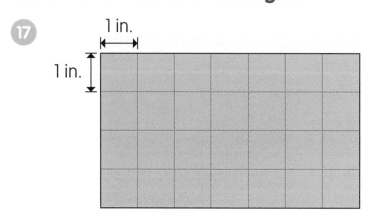

1 in.

1 in.

18

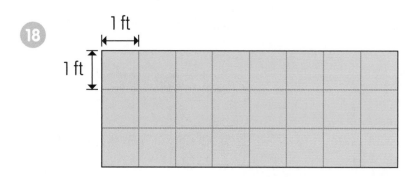

1 ft

1 ft

Use a centimeter ruler or inch ruler to measure the sides of each figure. Then, find the perimeter of each figure.

19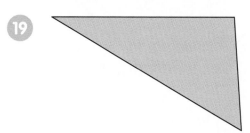

Perimeter = _____ cm

20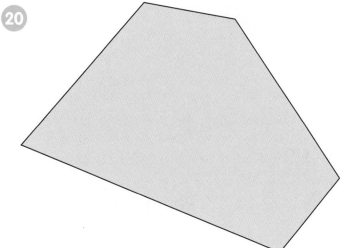

Perimeter = _____ in.

Find the perimeter of each figure in the correct unit.
Each figure is not drawn to scale.

21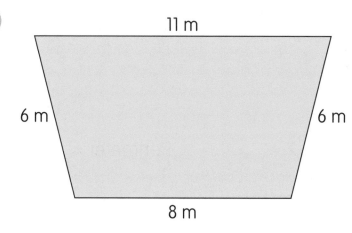

11 m

6 m   6 m   Perimeter = _____

8 m

22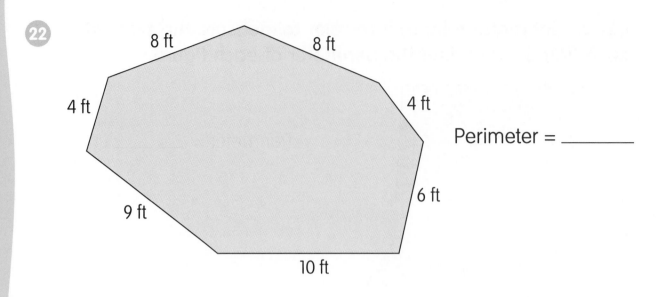

Perimeter = _____

23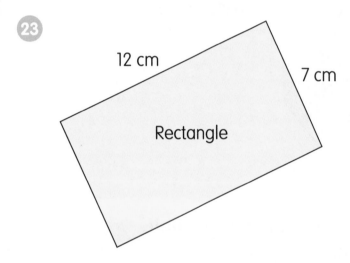

12 cm

7 cm

Rectangle

Perimeter = _____

24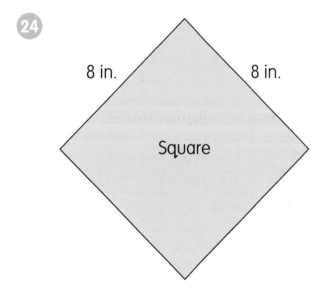

8 in.

8 in.

Square

Perimeter = _____

Draw a figure that has the same perimeter as the given figure. Then, find the area of each figure. The figure is not drawn to scale.

25

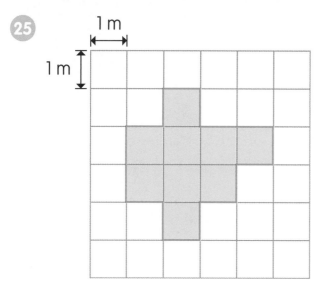

Area = _____ m²

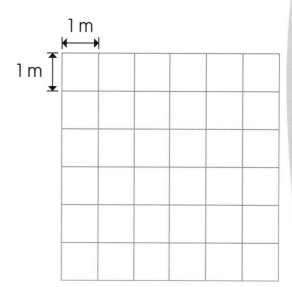

Area = _____ m²

Solve.

26 Audrey sticks some lace along the edges of a square card.
The square card has a side length of 6 inches.
What is the total length of lace Audrey uses?

6 in.

27) The length of a rectangular board is twice its width.
The perimeter of the board is 18 feet.
What is the width of the board?

28) Amari cuts out a piece of paper in the shape below.
The perimeter of the shape is 54 centimeters.
What is the length of the unknown side?

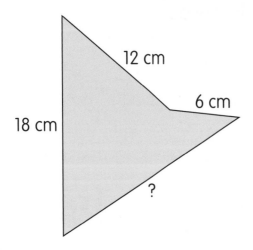

12 cm

6 cm

18 cm

?

29 Andrew ran around his neighborhood.
The figure shows the path he took.
Find the unknown length if he ran a total of 360 meters.

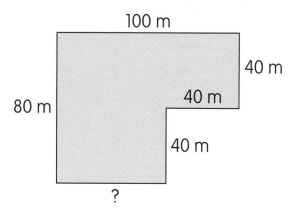

100 m

40 m

40 m

80 m

40 m

?

30 Paulina used 32 inches of lace to paste around the edges of four square cards. Find the side length of each card.

Assessment Prep

Answer each question.

31 A flower bed is in the shape of a rectangle.
It is 10 meters long and 6 meters wide.
What is the area of the flower bed?

  Ⓐ 16 square meters

  Ⓑ 30 square meters

  Ⓒ 32 square meters

  Ⓓ 60 square meters

32 Franco wants to carpet the floor of his rectangular bedroom.
His bedroom is 12 feet long and 10 feet wide.
What is the perimeter of the carpet Franco needs?

33 Ms. Scott drew a model of her bakery.

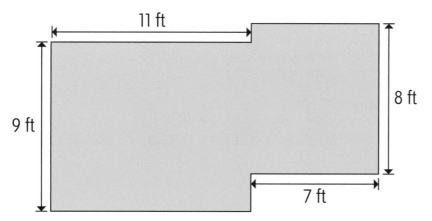

What is the area of her bakery?
Give your answer in square feet.
Explain how you found the answer.

34 The figures show the side lengths of some rectangular pieces of paper.

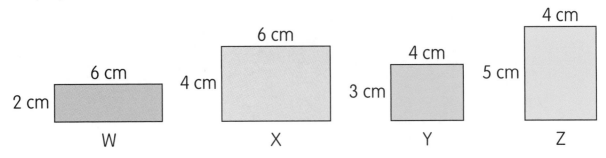

Part A
Which two rectangles have the same area?

Part B
Rectangles X and Z were pasted side by side to form a new shape.

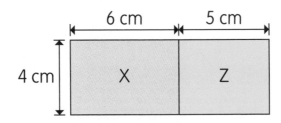

Landon uses (6 + 5) × 4 to find the total area of the new shape.
Aisha uses (6 × 4) + (5 × 4) to find the total area.
Are they correct? Why?

Name: _____ Date: _____

A Design Contest

Lincoln Elementary School is holding a design contest for its new garden. Vanessa and Silas want to join the contest. They each use grid paper to make their designs.

Vanessa's design:

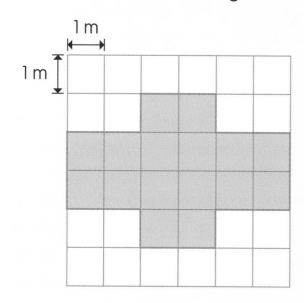

Silas's design:

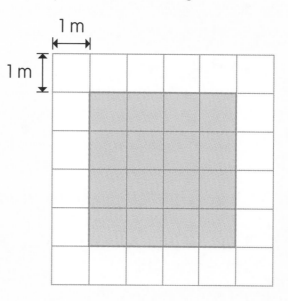

1 Silas thinks that his design should win because it has a larger area for planting. Is he correct? Explain your answer.

2 Vanessa thinks that her design should win because it has a greater perimeter. Is she correct? Explain your answer.

3 The winning design is rectangular in shape.
The length of the rectangular design is 3 times its width.
Its perimeter is 16 meters.
What is the length and width of the rectangular design?

Rubric

Point(s)	Level	My Performance
7–8	4	• Most of my answers are correct. • I showed complete understanding of what I have learned. • I used the correct strategies to solve the problems. • I explained my answers and mathematical thinking clearly and completely.
5–6.5	3	• Some of my answers are correct. • I showed some understanding of what I have learned. • I used some correct strategies to solve the problems. • I explained my answers and mathematical thinking clearly.
3–4.5	2	• A few of my answers are correct. • I showed little understanding of what I have learned. • I used a few correct strategies to solve the problems. • I explained some of my answers and mathematical thinking clearly.
0–2.5	1	• A few of my answers are correct. • I showed little or no understanding of what I have learned. • I used a few strategies to solve the problems. • I did not explain my answers and mathematical thinking clearly.

Teacher's Comments

How do you use a timeline to represent the start time, end time, and elapsed time of an activity?

Name: _____ Date: _____

Skip counting by 5s to tell time

Count by 5s.

5 10 15 20 25 30 35

The time is 35 minutes after 1 o'clock.
It is one thirty-five.
It can also be written as 1:35.

▶ **Quick Check**

Fill in each missing number.
Then, write each time in words.

1

The time is _____ minutes after 9 o'clock.

The time is _____.

2

The time is _____ minutes after 3 o'clock.

The time is _____.

Tell the time on each clock.

3

The time is _____.

4

The time is _____.

Telling time using A.M. and P.M.

A.M. shows the time after midnight but before noon.
P.M. shows the time after noon but before midnight.

30 minutes after 7
7:30

Camila goes to school at 7:30 A.M.
She takes her dinner at 7:30 P.M.

▶ **Quick Check**

Complete each sentence with A.M. or P.M.

5

Gavin eats his breakfast
at 7:05 _____.

6

Gavin goes to bed
at 9:20 _____.

Telling time to the hour or half hour

1 hour later

8:00 A.M. is 1 hour after 7:00 A.M.
7:00 A.M. is 1 hour before 8:00 A.M.

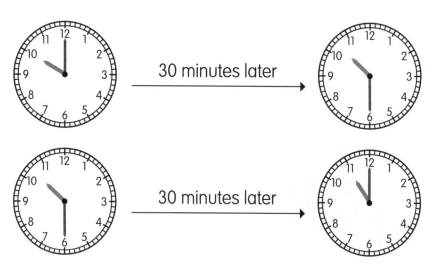

30 minutes later

30 minutes later

10.30 P.M. is 30 minutes or half an hour after 10:00 P.M.
10.30 P.M. is 30 minutes or half an hour before 11:00 P.M.

▶ **Quick Check**

Write each time using A.M. **or** P.M.

7 1 hour after 2:00 P.M. is _____.

8 1 hour before 11:00 A.M. is _____.

9 30 minutes after 11:30 A.M. is _____.

10 Half an hour before 5:30 P.M. is _____.

Telling Time

Learning Objectives:
- Tell time to the minute.
- Use the terms "past" and "to" to tell time.

New Vocabulary
past
to

**THINK**

Savannah tells Alonso that the time shown on her watch is 9:30 A.M.
Alonso says that she made a mistake.
What is the likely mistake that Savannah has made?
What could the correct time be?

ENGAGE

1. What is something you might do at 8:00 A.M.?
   What about 8:00 P.M.?
   What is the difference between A.M. and P.M.?

2. Use 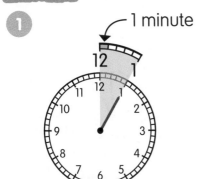 to show the time 8:05.
   What is something you might do at 8:05?
   Share your thinking with your partner.
   Write the time in words.

LEARN Tell time to the nearest minute using "past"

1

1 minute

Each small mark stands for 1 minute.

The minute hand shows 5 minutes.

2 Students are in the school hall at 9:12 A.M. for an assembly.

It is 12 minutes after 9 o'clock.

You can also say the time is 12 minutes past 9.

The time is nine twelve.

TRY Practice telling time to the nearest minute using "past"

Use the clock to find each missing answer.

1

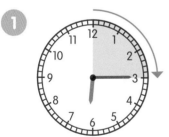

The time is six fifteen.

It is _____ minutes after 6.

6:15 is _____ minutes past 6.

2

  a Write the time in words.

   The time is _____.

  b It is _____ minutes past _____.

3

  a Write the time in words.

   The time is _____.

  b It is _____ minutes past _____.

Write the time on each clock in two ways.

4

  The time is _____.
  It can also be written as _____.

5

  The time is _____.
  It can also be written as _____.

Write each time in a different way.

6 5 minutes past 11 is _____.

7 13 minutes past 6 is _____.

Fill in each blank.

8 3:20 is _____ minutes past _____.

9 8:14 is _____ minutes past _____.

ENGAGE

1. Show 5 minutes past 1 on and write the time in two ways.

2. Now, show 5 minutes to 1 on and write the time in two ways.

LEARN Tell time to the nearest minute using "to"

1. The Sanchez family are having their dinner at 7:48 P.M.

The time is seven forty-eight.

60 − 48 = 12

It is 12 minutes before 8 o'clock.

You can also say the time is 12 minutes to 8.

Math Talk

When do you use "past" and "to" to tell time?

Work in groups of four.

Activity 1   Telling time to the nearest minute using "past" and "to"

(1) Use to show 21 minutes past 1.

(2) Change the time to show 21 minutes to 1.

(3) Describe how the minute hand and the hour hand have changed.

Activity 2   Understanding the duration of one minute

(1) Guess how many triangles you can draw in one minute.

I think I can draw _____ triangles in one minute.

(2) Ask your partner to time you as you draw as many triangles as you can in one minute.

TRY Practice telling time to the nearest minute using "to"

Use the clock to find each missing answer.

1

The time is five forty-five.

It is _____ minutes to 6.

5:45 is _____ minutes to 6.

2

a Write the time in words.

The time is _____.

b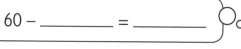

60 – _____ = _____

It is _____ minutes to _____.

3

a Write the time in words.

The time is _____.

b

60 – _____ = _____

It is _____ minutes to _____.

Write the time on each clock in two ways.

4

The time is _____.

It can also be written as _____.

5

The time is _____.

It can also be written as _____.

Write each time in a different way.

6 5 minutes to 11 is _____.

7 12 minutes to 8 is _____.

8 23 minutes to 5 is _____.

Fill in each blank.

9 12:35 is _____ minutes to _____.

10 2:51 is _____ minutes to _____.

11 10:43 is _____ minutes to _____.

SHOW AND TELL TIME!

What you need:

Players: 4 to 8

Materials:

What to do:

1 Form two groups, Group 1 and Group 2.

2 Group 1 shows a time by moving the hands on the .

3 Group 2 tells the time in two ways.

4 Group 1 checks the answer.
Group 2 gets 1 point for each correct answer.

5 Each group takes turns showing and telling the time.

Who is the winner?

The group with the most points wins.

Name: _____   Date: _____

INDEPENDENT PRACTICE

Write the time on each clock using past or to.

1

The time is _____.

2

The time is _____.

3

The time is _____.

4

The time is _____.

5
86:15

The time is _____.

6
88:48

The time is _____.

7 `12:37`   The time is _____.

8 `1:08`   The time is _____.

Write each time in a different way.

9 7 minutes past 9 is _____.

10 7 minutes to 9 is _____.

11 21 minutes past 3 is _____.

12 21 minutes to 3 is _____.

Fill in each blank.

13 4:06 is _____ minutes past _____.

14 7:52 is _____ minutes to _____.

15 10:13 is _____ minutes past _____.

16 2:41 is _____ minutes to _____.

2 Converting Hours and Minutes

Learning Objective:
• Convert hours and minutes to minutes and vice versa.

New Vocabulary
hour (h)
minute (min)

THINK

Jordan and Madison each converted 150 minutes to hours and minutes.
Who is correct? Why?

Jordan's method:
150 min = 100 min + 50 min
        = 1 h 50 min

Madison's method:
150 min = 60 min + 60 min + 30 min
        = 2 h 30 min

ENGAGE

Move the minute hand round a  twice.
How many minutes does the hand pass?
What strategy did you use?

LEARN Convert hours to minutes

1. Dara rides his bicycle for 2 hours.
   How many minutes are there in 2 hours?

   2 h = 60 + 60
       = 120 min

   1 h = 60 min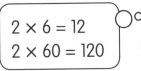

   You can also multiply to convert hours to minutes.

   2 h = 2 × 60
       = 120 min

   2 × 6 = 12
   2 × 60 = 120

   There are 120 minutes in 2 hours.

   > h stands for hour. 1 h is read as one hour.
   > min stands for minutes. 30 min is read as thirty minutes.

2 Addison plays basketball for 1 hour 10 minutes.
How many minutes does she play basketball for?

1 h 10 min $<$ 1 h = 60 min
10 min

1 h 10 min = 60 min + 10 min
= 70 min

She plays basketball for 70 minutes.

TRY Practice converting hours to minutes

Fill in each missing number.

1

1 h 45 min $<$ _____ h
_____ min

2

3 h 40 min $<$ _____ h
_____ min

Write each time in minutes. Fill in each blank.

3 2 h 45 min

= _____ min + _____ min

= _____ min

| 1 h = 60 min |
| 2 h = 2 × _____ |
| = _____ min |

4 4 h 28 min

= _____ min + _____ min

= _____ min

| 1 h = 60 min |
| 4 h = 4 × _____ |
| = _____ min |

Write each time in minutes. Fill in each blank.

5 3 h 54 min = _____ min

6 4 h 33 min = _____ min

ENGAGE

1 How many minutes are there in

   a 1 hour,   **b** 2 hours,   **c** 3 hours?

Describe your strategy with your partner.

2 Camila read a book for 2 hours 45 minutes in the morning. How long did she read for in minutes?

LEARN Convert minutes to hours and minutes

1 Ms. Wilson takes 135 minutes to mow the lawn. How many hours and minutes does she take to mow the lawn?

$$135 \text{ min} < \begin{array}{l} 120 \text{ min} = 2 \text{ h} \\ 15 \text{ min} \end{array}$$

$$135 \text{ min} = 120 \text{ min} + 15 \text{ min}$$
$$= 2 \text{ h } 15 \text{ min}$$

1 h = 60 min
2 h = 120 min ✓
3 h = 180 min

She takes 2 hours 15 minutes to mow the lawn.

TRY Practice converting minutes to hours and minutes

Write each time in hours and minutes.

1 90 min = _____ min + _____ min

        = _____ h _____ min

2 130 min = _____ min + _____ min

        = _____ h _____ min

3 208 min = _____ h _____ min

TIME BINGO!

What you need:

Players: 4

Materials: Time cards, Bingo board

What to do:

1. Form two groups, Group 1 and Group 2.

2. Group 1 draws a card from the stack of Time Cards.

3. A player from Group 1 writes the time in another form to complete the equation.

4. Group 1 makes an ✗ on the grid with the correct answer.

5. Each group takes turns to play.
Group 2 marks their answers on the grid with an O.

Who is the winner?

The first group to mark three correct answers in a straight line on the bingo board wins.

INDEPENDENT PRACTICE

Write each time in minutes.

1 1 h 25 min = _____ min

2 2 h 40 min = _____ min

3 3 h 3 min = _____ min

4 4 h 19 min = _____ min

Write each time in hours and minutes.

5 80 min = _____ h _____ min

6 165 min = _____ h _____ min

7 203 min = _____ h _____ min

8 369 min = _____ h _____ min

Write each time in hours and minutes.

9 Connor took 1 hour 25 minutes to cycle around his neighborhood. How many minutes are there in 1 hour 25 minutes?

10 A concert was 2 hours 9 minutes long.
How many minutes are there in 2 hours 9 minutes?

11 Ravi spent 74 minutes writing his essay.
How many hours and minutes are there in 74 minutes?

12 Mr. King drove from his home to the next town in 198 minutes.
How many hours and minutes are there in 198 minutes?

3 Elapsed Time

Learning Objectives:
- Find end time, start time, or elapsed time.
- Solve real-world problems involving time.

New Vocabulary
elapsed time
timeline

THINK

Adeline takes a plane from Miami to Boston at 8:15 A.M.
There are flights from Boston to Miami every 3 hours from 8:15 A.M.
Adeline wants to return to Miami on the same day.
The flight takes 3 hours 40 minutes each way.
What time is the latest flight she can take?

ENGAGE

Use a  to show how much time has passed for the following.

a from 1:00 P.M. to 3:00 P.M.
b from 12:45 P.M. to 3:00 P.M.
c from 1:00 P.M. to 3:25 P.M.
d from 12:50 P.M. to 3:30 P.M.

LEARN Find elapsed time given the start and end time

1. Anthony's soccer practice started at 3:00 P.M.
It ended at 5:00 P.M.
How long was his soccer practice?

Start:

Use a timeline to find elapsed time.

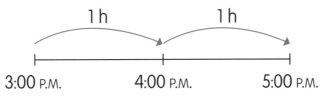

3:00 P.M.   4:00 P.M.   5:00 P.M.

End:

His soccer practice was 2 hours long.

Elapsed time is the amount of time that has passed between the start and the end of an activity.

2 Carolina started her dinner at 6:45 P.M.
She finished at 7:20 P.M.
How long did she take to finish her dinner?

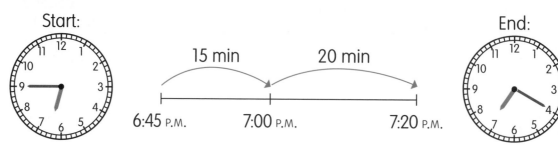

Start: 15 min   20 min   End:

6:45 P.M.   7:00 P.M.   7:20 P.M.

15 + 20 = 35

She took 35 minutes to finish her dinner.

3 Kayla and Antonio went to a fair.
They arrived at 7:50 P.M. and left the fair at 9:15 P.M.
How long were they at the fair?

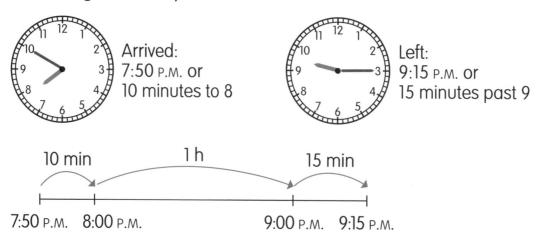

Arrived:
7:50 P.M. or
10 minutes to 8

Left:
9:15 P.M. or
15 minutes past 9

10 min   1 h   15 min

7:50 P.M.   8:00 P.M.   9:00 P.M.   9:15 P.M.

10 min + 1 h + 15 min = 1 h 25 min

They were at the fair for 1 hour 25 minutes.

Work in groups of four.

① Take turns telling your group the last time you did each activity. Include the time you think you started and ended each one.

Reading a story

Playing a game

Having lunch

② Write down your start time and end time for each activity.

Reading a story	Playing a game	Having lunch
Start time: _____	Start time: _____	Start time: _____
End time: _____	End time: _____	End time: _____

③ Draw a timeline for each activity to find the elapsed time.

④ Answer the following questions.
   a   Who takes the longest time to read a story?
   b   Who takes the shortest time to have lunch?
   c   Who takes the shortest time to play a game?

TRY Practice finding elapsed time given the start and end time

Find each elapsed time. Draw a timeline to help you.

1 6:00 A.M. to 10:00 A.M. _____

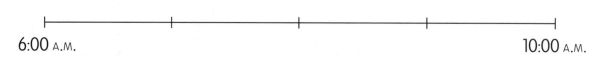

6:00 A.M.   10:00 A.M.

2 11:13 A.M. to 2:13 P.M. _____

3 8:35 P.M. to 9:10 P.M. _____

8:35 P.M.   9:00 P.M.   9:10 P.M.

4 3:25 A.M. to 4:12 A.M. _____

5 Noon to 4:55 P.M. _____

12 noon   4:00 P.M.   4:55 P.M.

6 11:43 A.M. to 2:27 P.M. _____

11:43 A.M. 12 noon   2:00 P.M.   2:27 P.M.

7 A train left Town P at 7:30 A.M.
It arrived at Town Q at 11:44 A.M.
How long was the trip?

```
├──────────────────────┼──────┤
7:30 A.M.          11:30 A.M.  11:44 A.M.
```

The trip was _____ hours _____ minutes long.

8 Santino and Rafaela went to a zoo.
They arrived at 8:31 A.M. and left at 10:16 A.M.
How long were they at the zoo?

```
├────────┼──────────────────┼────┤
8:31 A.M.   9:00 A.M.      10:00 A.M.  10:16 A.M.
```

_____ min + _____ h + _____ min = _____ h _____ min

They were at the zoo for _____ hour _____ minutes.

9 Samantha left her house at 2:22 P.M.
She reached home at 5:13 P.M.
How long was she out for?

```
├────────┼──────────────────┼──┤
2:22 P.M.                      5:13 P.M.
```

_____ min + _____ h + _____ min = _____ h _____ min

She was out for _____ hours _____ minutes.

ENGAGE

Ang started doing his homework at 4:00 P.M.
He spent 1 hour doing his homework.
At what time did he finish?
Describe how you found the answer to your partner.

LEARN Find end time given the start and elapsed time

1 After a party, Indira cleaned her house.
She started at 10:30 P.M. and finished in 1 hour 45 minutes.
At what time did she finish cleaning the house?

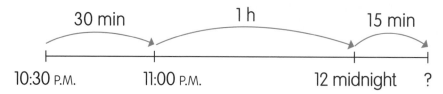

When you pass midnight,
P.M. becomes A.M.

30 minutes after 10:30 P.M. is 11:00 P.M.

1 hour after 11:00 P.M. is midnight.

15 minutes after midnight is 12:15 A.M.

She finished cleaning the house at 12:15 A.M.

Check
1 hour before 12:15 A.M. is 11:15 P.M.
45 minutes before 11:15 P.M. is 10:30 P.M.

TRY Practice finding end time given the start and elapsed time

Draw a timeline to find each end time.

1 A movie starts at 7:15 P.M.
It lasts 2 hours 15 minutes.
At what time does the movie end?

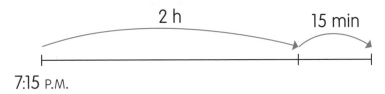

The movie ends at _____.

2 Mr. Harris took 2 hours 33 minutes to bake pies.
He started baking them at 10:40 A.M.
At what time did Mr. Harris finish baking the pies?

Mr. Harris finished baking the pies at _____.

3 Ms. Gomez spent 3 hours 57 minutes tidying her house.
She started tidying at 1:15 P.M.
At what time did Ms. Gomez finish tidying her house?

Ms. Gomez finished tidying her house at _____.

ENGAGE

Describe to your partner how a timeline could
help you to find 1 hour 30 minutes before 6:00 P.M.
Now, draw the timeline. Did your method work?
Explain your thinking to your partner.

LEARN Find start time given the end and elapsed time

1   Katherine finished painting a sign at 3:00 P.M.
    She took 1 hour 50 minutes to paint the sign.
    At what time did she begin painting?

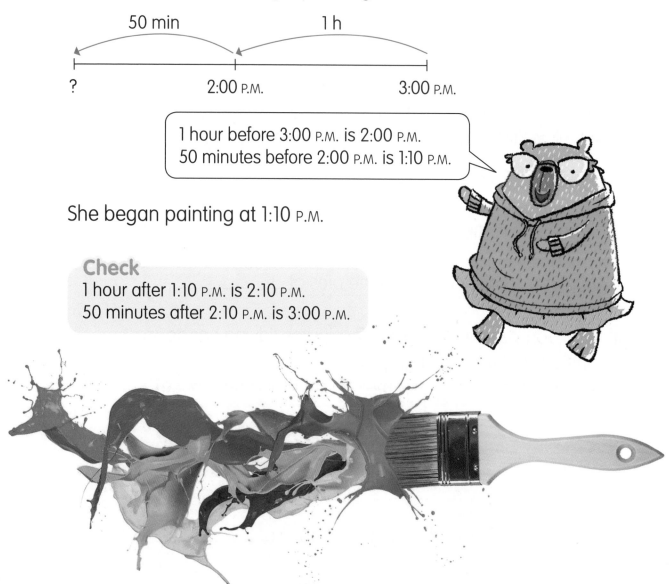

50 min   1 h

?   2:00 P.M.   3:00 P.M.

1 hour before 3:00 P.M. is 2:00 P.M.
50 minutes before 2:00 P.M. is 1:10 P.M.

She began painting at 1:10 P.M.

Check
1 hour after 1:10 P.M. is 2:10 P.M.
50 minutes after 2:10 P.M. is 3:00 P.M.

Draw a timeline to find each start time.

1 Victoria sat for a Math quiz.
The quiz was 1 hour 15 minutes long and ended at 10:45 A.M.
At what time did the quiz begin?

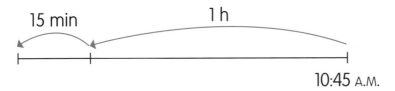

15 min   1 h

10:45 A.M.

The quiz began at _____.

2 Mr. Moore took 2 hours 40 minutes to drive from Town A to Town B.
He arrived at Town B at 2:25 P.M.
At what time did he start from Town A?

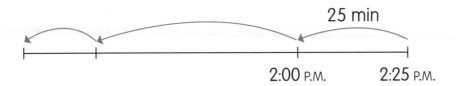

25 min

2:00 P.M.   2:25 P.M.

He started from Town A at _____.

3 Yong finished drawing a picture at 12:16 P.M.
He took 3 hours 42 minutes to complete the picture.
At what time did he start drawing?

12 noon   12:16 P.M.

He started drawing at _____.

ENGAGE

Dominic left the school for the beach at 11:45 A.M.
After some time, Ivanna started her journey along the same route.
Both of them arrived at the beach at the same time.
Dominic took 1 hour 35 minutes to reach the beach.
If Ivanna took 15 minutes less for her journey,
at what time did she begin her journey?

LEARN Solve real-world problems involving time

1. Arianna spent 40 minutes doing her homework.
   She spent another 45 minutes practicing the piano.
   She finished her homework and piano practice at 5:30 P.M.
   At what time did Arianna begin doing her homework?

 Understand the problem.

> How long did she spend
> doing the two activities?
> At what time did she
> finish the activities?
> What do I need to find?

 Think of a plan.
I can draw a timeline.

STEP 3 Carry out the plan.

40 min + 45 min
= 85 min
= 1 h 25 min

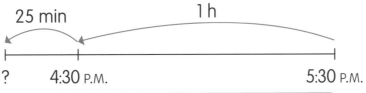

85 min $\diagup$ 60 min = 1 h
$\diagdown$ 25 min

Arianna spent a total of 1 hour 25 minutes doing her homework and practicing the piano.

25 min   1 h

?   4:30 P.M.   5:30 P.M.

1 hour before 5:30 P.M. is 4:30 P.M.
25 minutes before 4:30 P.M. is 4:05 P.M.

Arianna began doing her homework at 4:05 P.M.

STEP 4 Check the answer.
I can work backwards to check the time.

1 hour after 4:05 P.M. is 5:05 P.M.
25 minutes after 5:05 P.M. is 5:30 P.M.
My answer is correct.

2 Elijah arrives at a train station.
His watch shows the time as 6:45 A.M.
His watch is 20 minutes slow.

a   What is the actual time when he arrives at the train station?
b   The train arrives 10 minutes later.
     What is the actual time when the train arrives?

a

15 min   5 min

6:45 A.M.   7:00 A.M.   7:05 A.M.

The actual time when he arrives at the train station is 7:05 A.M.

b

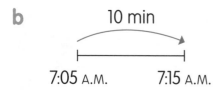

10 min

7:05 A.M.   7:15 A.M.

The actual time when the train arrives is 7:15 A.M.

3 A documentary was aired on the television network from 7:30 P.M.
It ended after 1 hour 45 minutes.
The daily news aired for 55 minutes after the documentary.
At what time did the daily news end?

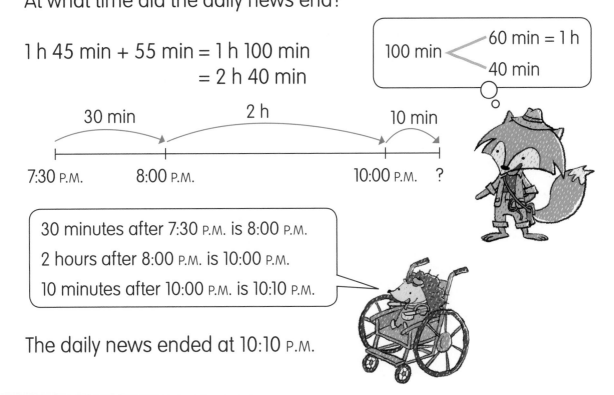

1 h 45 min + 55 min = 1 h 100 min
$\qquad\qquad\qquad\quad$ = 2 h 40 min

100 min $\Big\langle$ 60 min = 1 h
$\qquad\qquad$ 40 min

30 min $\qquad$ 2 h $\qquad$ 10 min

7:30 P.M. $\qquad$ 8:00 P.M. $\qquad\qquad$ 10:00 P.M. $\quad$?

30 minutes after 7:30 P.M. is 8:00 P.M.

2 hours after 8:00 P.M. is 10:00 P.M.

10 minutes after 10:00 P.M. is 10:10 P.M.

The daily news ended at 10:10 P.M.

Hands-on Activity Solving real-world problems involving time

Work in groups.

1 Bring a television program schedule with your favorite
television program.

2 Take turns to tell each other about your favorite television program.
What is its start time? What time does the program end?

Favorite television program: _____

Start time: _____

End time: _____

(3) Use the information in the program schedule to create a real-world problem.

Example:
It is 2:25 P.M.
Science Corner starts at 4:30 P.M.
How long do I have to wait to watch Science Corner?

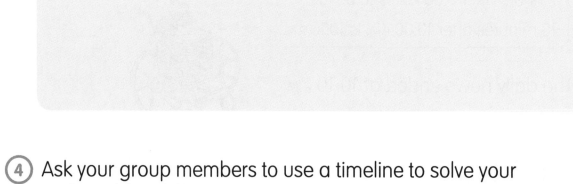

(4) Ask your group members to use a timeline to solve your real-world problem.

TRY Practice solving real-world problems involving time

Solve. Draw a timeline to help you.

1. On Monday, a storm started at 5:23 P.M. and ended at 9:18 P.M.
   On Tuesday a storm occurred again.
   It lasted for 3 hours 20 minutes.
   a How long did the storm last on Monday?
   b How much longer did the storm last on Monday than on Tuesday?

   a

   5:23 P.M.   6:00 P.M.

   _____ min + _____ h + _____ min

   = _____ h _____ min

   The storm lasted _____ hours _____ minutes on Monday.

   b _____ h _____ min – _____ h _____ min

   = _____ min

   The storm lasted _____ minutes
   longer on Monday than on Tuesday.

   Subtract the hours first.
   Then, subtract the minutes.

2 A chef starts work at 8:45 A.M.
He usually works for 8 hours.
Today, he leaves a half hour earlier.
At what time does he leave the restaurant?

_____ h – _____ min = _____ h _____ min   (8 h = ____ h ____ min)

He works for _____ hours _____ minutes today.

|———————————————————————————————|————————|

8:45 A.M.

He leaves the restaurant at _____.

3 Ms. Clark drove 1 hour 34 minutes from Town X to Town Y.
Then, she drove another 2 hours 47 minutes from Town Y to
Town Z. She reached Town Z at 7:15 P.M.
At what time did she leave Town X?

INDEPENDENT PRACTICE

Find each end time.

1 2 hours after 7:00 P.M. is _____.

2 3 hours after 2:43 A.M. is _____.

3 36 minutes after 9:00 P.M. is _____.

4 28 minutes after 1:02 A.M. is _____.

Find each start time.

5 1 hour before 12:00 A.M. is _____.

6 3 hours before 8:19 P.M. is _____.

7 20 minutes before 3:00 P.M. is _____.

8 14 minutes before 10:19 A.M. is _____.

Find each elapsed time.
Draw a timeline to help you.

9 5:25 P.M. to 5:45 P.M. _____

10 7:54 A.M. to 9:54 A.M. _____

11 4:27 P.M to 5:10 P.M. _____

12 10:31 P.M. to midnight _____

13 1:53 A.M. to 4:28 A.M. _____

Solve. Draw a timeline to help you.

14 Christian went to school for a band concert.
He arrived at school at 7:15 P.M. according to his watch.
His watch was 30 minutes fast.

    a   What was the actual time when he arrived at school?

    b   He arrived just in time for the concert.
          The actual time the concert ended was at 9:00 P.M.
          How long did the concert last?

15 Mr. Torres was on a flight to Chicago.
The plane landed at the airport at 11:52 A.M.
He waited 45 minutes for his luggage and another 28 minutes for his wife to pick him up. At what time did his wife pick him up?

16 Angel cycled for 4 hours 30 minutes.
Josiah cycled for 1 hour 45 minutes less than Angel.
Josiah finished cycling at 6:22 P.M.
At what time did he start cycling?

Name: _____ Date: _____

Mathematical Habit 4 Use mathematical models

1. The steps for finding the elapsed time from 10:20 A.M. to 1:30 P.M. are not in order. Put them in the correct order.

   a   Find the elapsed time from 10:20 A.M. to 11:00 A.M.

   b   Mark the hours between the two endpoints.

   c   Add the elapsed time.

   d   Find the elapsed time from 11:00 A.M. to 1:00 P.M.

   e   Find the elapsed time from 1:00 P.M. to 1:30 P.M.

   f   Mark the start time and the end time on the timeline.

   g   Draw the timeline.

   STEP 1 _____   STEP 2 _____

   STEP 3 _____   STEP 4 _____

   STEP 5 _____   STEP 6 _____

   STEP 7 _____

2. List the steps to find the elapsed time from 1:15 P.M. to 11:20 P.M. Determine whether the steps are the same as 1.

   STEP 1 _____   STEP 2 _____

   STEP 3 _____   STEP 4 _____

   STEP 5 _____   STEP 6 _____

   STEP 7 _____

Problem Solving with Heuristics

1 **Mathematical Habit 2** Use mathematical reasoning

Miranda's watch is 15 minutes fast.
Her clock is 20 minutes slow.
If her watch shows the following time,
what time does her clock show?

watch

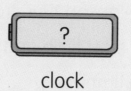

clock

2 **Mathematical Habit** 1 Persevere in solving problems

A bus arrives at a bus stop every 3 hours.
The first bus arrives at 7:15 A.M.
The last bus arrives before midnight.

a   At what time does the last bus arrive?

b   How many buses arrive at the bus stop in a day?

CHAPTER WRAP-UP

Time

Telling time

You can tell the time to the minute using an analog or a digital clock.

You can write the time using "past" and "to."

Example:
6:15 is the same as
15 minutes past 6.
5:40 is the same as
20 minutes to 6.

Converting Hours and Minutes

1 hour (h) = 60 minutes (min)

Convert time to minutes:
1 h 10 min = 60 min + 10 min
         = 70 min

Convert time to hours and minutes:
90 min = 60 min + 30 min
       = 1 h 30 min

Elapsed Time

Use a timeline to find elapsed time, start time, and end time.

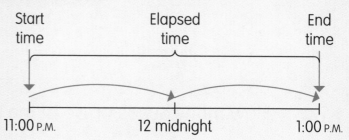

Start time   Elapsed time   End time

11:00 P.M.   12 midnight   1:00 P.M.

Find the elapsed time given the start and end time of an activity.

Find the end time given the start time and elapsed time of an activity.

Find the start time given the end time and elapsed time of an activity.

Adding time:
1 h 40 min + 1 h 27 min = 2 h 67 min
                        = 3 h 7 min

Subtracting time:
2 h 13 min − 1 h 38 min
= 1 h 73 min − 1 h 38 min
= 35 min

Name: _____ Date: _____

Write the time on each clock using past or to.

1  The time is _____.

2  The time is _____.

Write each time in a different way using A.M. or P.M.

3 23 minutes past 11 in the evening is _____.

4 3 minutes to 3 in the morning is _____.

Write each time in minutes.

5 2 h 40 min = _____ min

6 3 h 6 min = _____ min

7 4 h 18 min = _____ min

Write each time in hours and minutes.

8 98 min = _____ h _____ min

9 207 min = _____ h _____ min

10 360 min = _____ h _____ min

Solve. Draw a timeline to help you.

11 Jessica swam from 5:25 P.M. to 6:57 P.M. on Monday.
On Tuesday, she swam 30 minutes longer than on Monday.
How long did she swim for on Tuesday?

12 Madelyn left her house at 10:27 A.M.
She passed the library 45 minutes later.
She continued traveling and reached the mall at noon.
How long did she take to travel from the library to the mall?

13 Destiny finished her project in 2 hours 13 minutes.
Trevon finished the same project 38 minutes faster than Destiny.
He finished his project at 4:10 P.M.
At what time did Trevon start doing his project?

Assessment Prep

Answer each question.

14 Gael started jogging at 5:57 P.M. and stopped at 6:14 P.M.
How long did he jog for?

(A) 57 minutes

(B) 43 minutes

(C) 27 minutes

(D) 17 minutes

15 Jackson boarded a train at 11:43 A.M.
He got off the train 35 minutes later.
Which clock shows the time that Jackson got off the train?

Ⓐ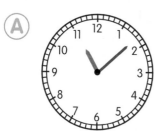

Ⓑ

Ⓒ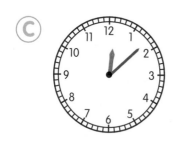

Ⓓ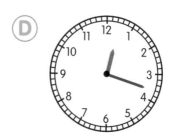

16 A train left Station A and traveled towards Stations B and C.
It passed Station B 54 minutes later.
The train took 47 minutes to travel from Station B to Station C.
It arrived at Station C at 5:08 P.M.
At what time did the train leave Station A?

Cooking for a Party

Mr. Reed was preparing some food for his daughter's party.
He prepared some soup, sandwiches, and pie.

1 Mr. Reed prepared his daughter's favorite pumpkin soup.

    a   The clock below shows the time he started boiling the soup.

At what time did he start boiling the soup?
Write your answer using past or to.

    b   Mr. Reed took the soup off the stove at 12 minutes past 11.
Fill in the clock to show the time.

c   How long did Mr. Reed boil the soup for? 12m, nhs

10:25 AM

2   Mr. Reed spent 12 minutes preparing the sandwiches.
He started preparing at 10:25 A.M.
Draw the missing hands on the clock to show the time
he finished preparing the sandwiches.
Then, complete the sentence below.

Mr. Reed finished preparing the sandwiches

at _10:25_ in the morning.

3 Mr. Reed wants the pie to be ready by 11:30 A.M.
The pie needs to be baked for 55 minutes.
What is the latest possible time he can put the pie in the oven?
Draw a timeline to help you.

Rubric

Point(s)	Level	My Performance
7–8	4	• Most of my answers are correct. • I showed complete understanding of what I have learned. • I used the correct strategies to solve the problems. • I explained my answers and mathematical thinking clearly and completely.
5–6	3	• Some of my answers are correct. • I showed some understanding of what I have learned. • I used some correct strategies to solve the problems. • I explained my answers and mathematical thinking clearly.
3–4	2	• A few of my answers are correct. • I showed little understanding of what I have learned. • I used a few correct strategies to solve the problems. • I explained some of my answers and mathematical thinking clearly.
0–2	1	• A few of my answers are correct. • I showed little or no understanding of what I have learned. • I used a few strategies to solve the problems. • I did not explain my answers and mathematical thinking clearly.

Teacher's Comments

Chapter 11

Graphs and Line Plots

How can you organize data?

Name: _____ Date: _____

Using graphs to show data

Kimberly has the following solid shapes.

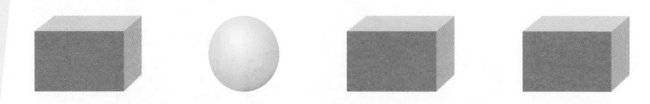

She made this tally chart to show the number of each solid shape.

Type of Solid Shapes	Name	Tally	Number of Solid Shapes
	Cube	|||||	5
	Cylinder	|||	3
	Rectangular Prism	||||| |||||	10
	Sphere	||	2
	Pyramid	||||	4

Then, Kimberly made a picture graph to show the data.

Kimberly's Solid Shapes

Cube	Cylinder	Rectangular Prism	Sphere	Pyramid
☆☆☆☆☆	☆☆☆	☆☆☆☆☆ ☆☆☆☆☆	☆☆	☆☆☆☆

Key: Each ☆ stands for 1 solid shape.

She also used a bar graph to show the data.

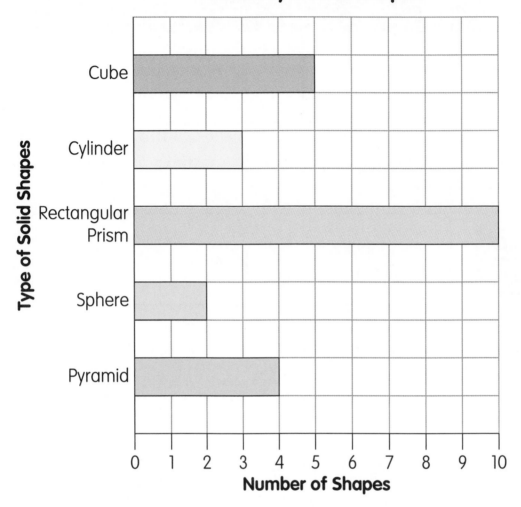

Kimberly's Solid Shapes

She has 5 cubes, 3 cylinders, 10 rectangular prisms, 2 spheres, and 4 pyramids.

5 + 3 + 10 + 2 + 4 = 24

Kimberly has a total of 24 solid shapes.

▶ **Quick Check**

The pictures show the number of each animal at a zoo.

Fill in the tally chart.
Then, use the data to complete each graph.

Type of Animals	Tally	Number of Animals
(bear)	┼┼┼┤ ┤┤┤	7
(penguin)	┼┼┼┤ ┼┼┼┤ ┤┤	9
(sheep)	┼┼┼┤ ┤┤	6
(giraffe)	┼┼┼┤ ┤┤┤	7

Animals at the Zoo

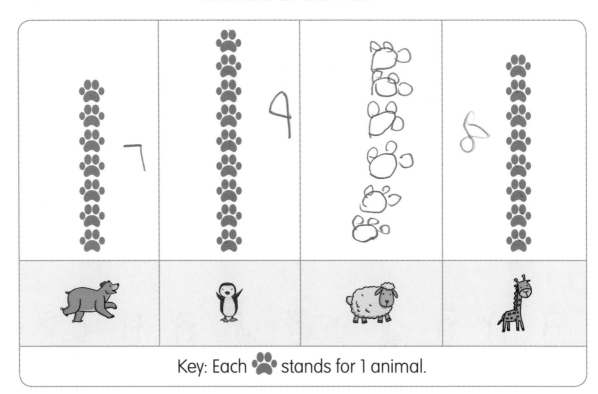

Key: Each 🐾 stands for 1 animal.

Animals at the Zoo

Type of Animals

Number of Animals

0 1 2 3 4 5 6 7 8 9 10 11 12

1 Making Picture Graphs with Scales

Learning Objectives:
- Make picture graphs with scales to present data.
- Read and interpret picture graphs with scales.

THINK

Farmer Alexander has 3 times as many ducks as cows on his farm.
There are 4 times as many chickens as cows on his farm.
If there are 8 cows on his farm, show two ways you can represent the number of animals in a picture graph.

ENGAGE

Take 100 🎲 of three different colors.
There should be more than 30 🎲 of each color.
How would you make a picture graph to show the different colors?

LEARN Make picture graphs with scales

① Adriana buys four types of fruit.
She uses a picture graph to show the number of each type of fruit she has bought.

Type of Fruit

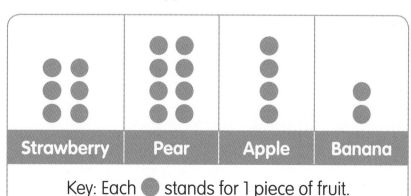

Key: Each ● stands for 1 piece of fruit.

> 1 ● stands for 1 piece of fruit. You can read this picture graph by counting the ●.

Adriana redraws the picture graph.
Now, she uses 1 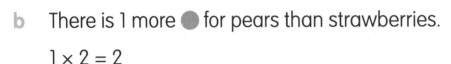 for 2 pieces of fruit.

Type of Fruit

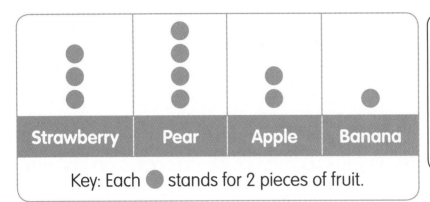

| Strawberry | Pear | Apple | Banana |

Key: Each ⬤ stands for 2 pieces of fruit.

> 1 ⬤ stands for 2 pieces of fruit. So, multiply the number of ⬤ by 2 to get the number of fruit.

a   There are 3 ⬤ for strawberries.

$3 \times 2 = 6$
There are 6 strawberries.

b   There is 1 more ⬤ for pears than strawberries.

$1 \times 2 = 2$
There are 2 more pears than strawberries.

c   There are 7 ⬤ for strawberries and pears.

$7 \times 2 = 14$
There are 14 strawberries and pears altogether.

d   Adriana buys 4 pieces of a fruit.

$4 \div 2 = 2$
There are 2 ⬤ for this fruit.
She buys 4 apples.

e   There are 2 fewer ⬤ for apples than pears.

$2 \times 2 = 4$
Adriana buys 4 fewer apples than pears.

2 The picture graph shows the number of bookmarks five children have.

Number of Bookmarks

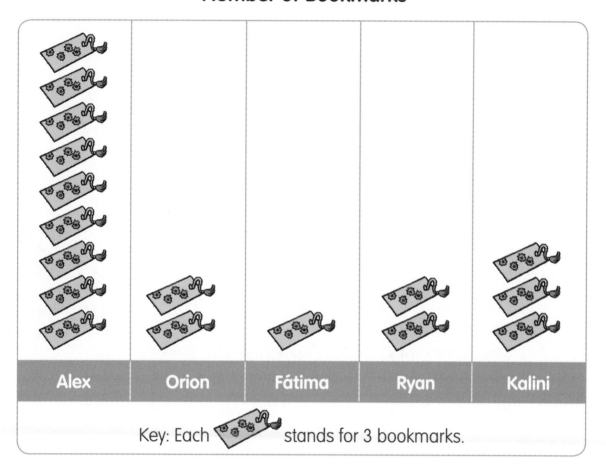

Key: Each [bookmark] stands for 3 bookmarks.

a How many bookmarks does Alex have?

There are 9 [bookmark] for Alex.

$9 \times 3 = 27$

Alex has 27 bookmarks.

b How many bookmarks does Orion have?

There are 2 [bookmark] for Orion.

$2 \times 3 = 6$

Orion has 6 bookmarks.

c How many bookmarks does Kalini have?

There are 3  for Kalini.

$3 \times 3 = 9$

Kalini has 9 bookmarks.

d How many more bookmarks does Ryan have than Fátima?

Ryan has 1 more than Fátima.

$1 \times 3 = 3$

Ryan has 3 more bookmarks than Fátima.

It is easy to compare data using a picture graph.

e Kalini has 6 bookmarks from Ms. Jones. The rest are from Mr. Cruz.
How many of Kalini's bookmarks are from Mr. Cruz?

$9 - 6 = 3$

3 of Kalini's bookmarks are from Mr. Cruz.

3 Mr. Nguyen has a farm.
He counts each type of animal on his farm.

He records the number of each type of animal he has.

Chicken	Turkey	Duck	Sheep	Horse
10	2	12	6	4

Mr. Nguyen draws a picture graph of his data.
He gives his graph a title.
He uses a ♡ to stand for 2 animals.
He has 5 types of animals.

He has 10 chickens.

$10 \div 2 = 5$

He draws 5 ♡ for chicken.

He has 2 turkeys.

$2 \div 2 = 1$

He draws 1 ♡ for turkey.

He continues to find the number of ♡ for duck, sheep, and horse.

Animals on Mr. Nguyen's Farm

		♡		
♡		♡		
♡		♡		
♡		♡	♡	
♡		♡	♡	♡
♡	♡	♡	♡	♡
Chicken	Turkey	Duck	Sheep	Horse

Key: Each ♡ stands for 2 animals.

Work in groups.

(1) Conduct a survey for the students in your class to find the favorite color of each student.

(2) Record your data in the tally chart.

Color	Tally	Number of Classmates

(3) Use ▲ to make the picture graph.

Favorite Colors

Key: Each ▲ stands for _____ classmates.

(4) Ask your classmates questions based on your picture graph.

TRY Practice making picture graphs with scales

The picture graph shows the favorite sports of a group of children.

Favorite Sports

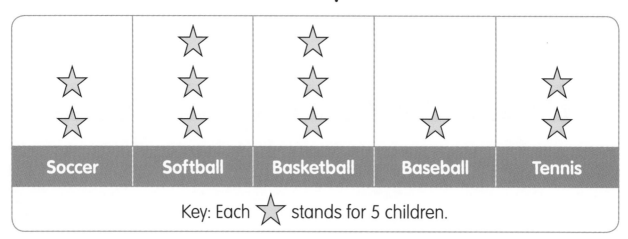

Key: Each ⭐ stands for 5 children.

Fill in each blank.

1. How many children like basketball?

   There are _____ ⭐ for basketball.

   _____ × _____ = _____

   _____ children like basketball.

2. How many children like softball and soccer in all?

   There are _____ ⭐ for softball and soccer in all.

   _____ × _____ = _____

   _____ children like softball and soccer in all.

3. How many more children like tennis than baseball?

   There is _____ more ⭐ for tennis than baseball.

   _____ × _____ = _____

   _____ more children like tennis than baseball.

The picture graph shows the types of animals a pet shop has.

Animals at a Pet Shop

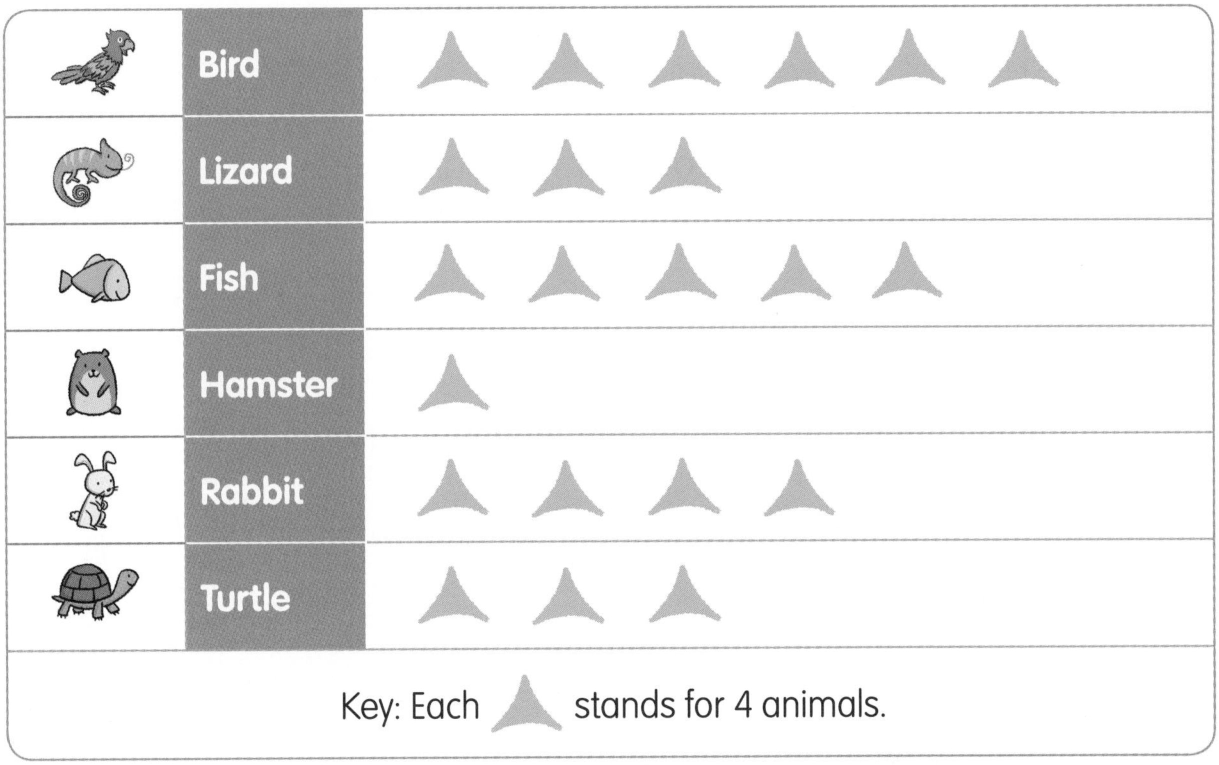

🦜	**Bird**	▲ ▲ ▲ ▲ ▲ ▲
🦎	**Lizard**	▲ ▲ ▲
🐟	**Fish**	▲ ▲ ▲ ▲ ▲
🐹	**Hamster**	▲
🐰	**Rabbit**	▲ ▲ ▲ ▲
🐢	**Turtle**	▲ ▲ ▲

Key: Each ▲ stands for 4 animals.

Fill in each blank.

④ The pet shop has _____ birds.

⑤ The pet shop has _____ lizards.

6 The pet shop has 20 _____.

7 There are _____ rabbits and turtles in all.

8 The pet shop has _____ more birds than hamsters.

Mathematical Habit 6 Use precise mathematical language

The picture graph shows the weather in April.

Weather in April

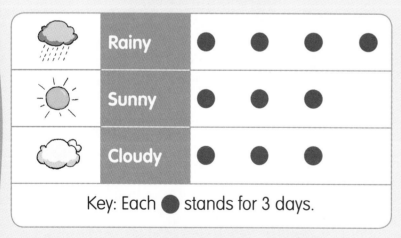

Key: Each ● stands for 3 days.

Make a story about the picture graph.
You may use the following words:

as many ... as   **more**   **fewer**

Name: _____ Date: _____

Jesus, Charlotte, Hunter, and Vicente went on a fishing trip.
They recorded the number of fish caught in the picture graph.

Number of Fish Caught

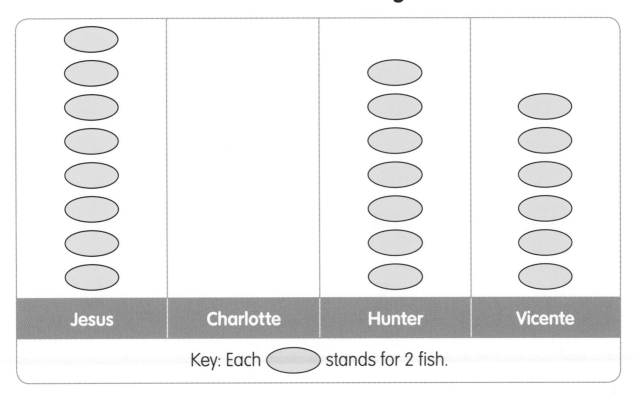

Use the data in the picture graph to answer each question.

1. Charlotte caught the same number of fish as Hunter.
   Complete the picture graph.

2. Jesus caught _____ fish.

3 Vicente caught _____ fish.

4 _____ caught 2 fewer fish than Jesus.

5 _____ caught the greatest number of fish.

6 _____ caught the least number of fish.

7 The children caught _____ fish in all.

A group of third graders counted the number of flowers in the garden. The picture graph shows the number of flowers of each color.

Flowers in the Garden

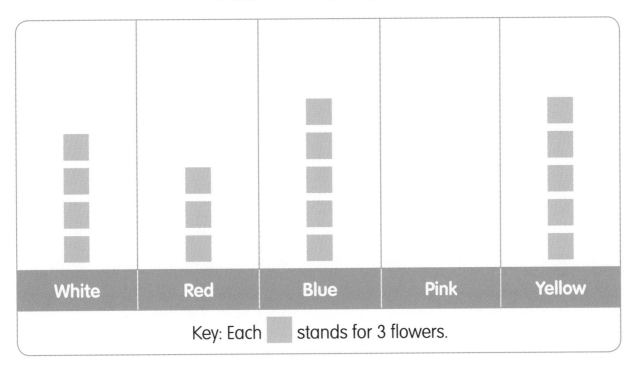

Key: Each ▮ stands for 3 flowers.

Use the data in the picture graph to answer each question.

8 They counted 21 pink flowers.
Complete the picture graph.

9 They counted _____ red flowers.

10 They counted _____ yellow flowers.

11 There were the same number of _____ and _____ flowers.

12 The greatest number of flowers were _____ in color.

13 The least number of flowers were _____ in color.

14 There were _____ more blue flowers than red flowers.

15 The third graders counted _____ flowers in all.

2 Making Bar Graphs with Scales

Learning Objective:
• Make bar graphs with scales to present data.

THINK

Jonathan has 30 paper cut-outs of different shapes. The bar graph shows the number of each shape he has. The bars for the squares and triangles are missing. What are the possible number of squares and triangles? Make a list.

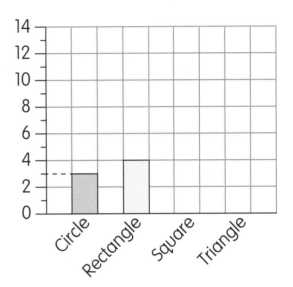

ENGAGE

Look at the picture.

How can you display the data using a bar graph?
What decisions do you need to make when drawing the bar graph?
Explain your thinking to your partner.

LEARN Make bar graphs from picture graphs

1 Four friends went for a nature walk.
The picture graph shows the number of butterflies each friend saw.

Number of Butterflies Seen

Juan	🦋🦋🦋🦋	4
Kylie	🦋🦋🦋🦋🦋🦋🦋🦋🦋🦋	10
Irene	🦋🦋🦋🦋🦋🦋🦋🦋	8
Caleb	🦋🦋🦋🦋🦋🦋	6

Key: Each 🦋 stands for 1 butterfly.

Look at this graph.

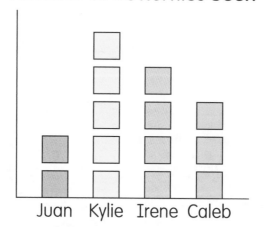

Number of Butterflies Seen

Juan   Kylie   Irene   Caleb

a How many butterflies does each ☐ stand for?

Each ☐ stands for 2 butterflies.

b Who saw the most number of butterflies?

Kylie saw the most number of butterflies.

2 Mariana uses the data to make a vertical bar graph.
A scale shows the value of the bars.
In this graph, the vertical axis or grid line is marked 0, 2, 4, 6, 8, 10, and 12. These markings represent the scale.

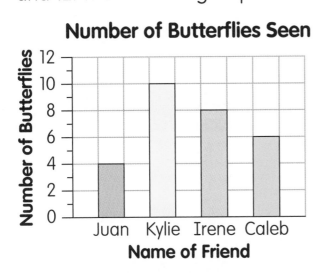

Number of Butterflies Seen

Like a picture graph, a bar graph is also useful for comparing data.

Then, Karina redraws the vertical graph as a horizontal graph.

Number of Butterflies Seen

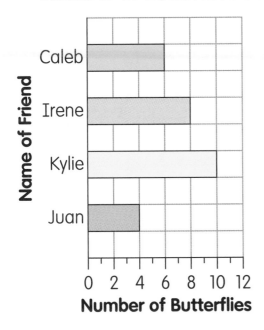

Karina's graph uses a scale of 2.
It starts with 0 and skips in twos.
The greatest number on the scale is 12 because it needs to include all the data.

Hands-on Activity Making a bar graph

Work in groups.

(1) Groups of students from King Elementary School took part in the school's field day.

The chart shows the number of medals won by each group.

Medals Won

Group	Evergreen	Birch	Maple	Gum	Bay
Number of Medals	10	14	18	12	16

Use the grid to make a bar graph that displays the data in the table. Give the bar graph a title.

Label the vertical and horizontal axes of the graph.

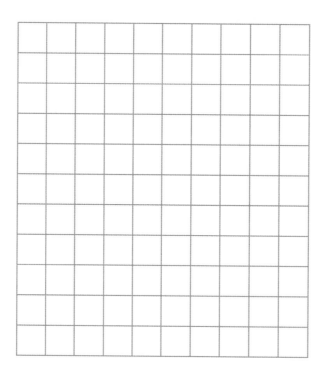

② **Mathematical Habit 6** Use precise mathematical language

Answer each question.

a   How did you decide on a scale for your graph? Explain.

b   What is the greatest number for your scale? Explain.

c   Only groups that won 10 or more medals are shown in the table. In all, 100 medals were won.
How many medals are not shown in the chart? Explain.

TRY Practice making bar graphs from picture graphs

Use the data in the tally chart to complete each graph.

Ian recorded the number of model cars that he and his friends collected in a tally chart.

Our Model Cars

Name	Tally	Number of Model Cars
Ian	卌 |	6
Anya	卌 |||	8
Axel	卌 卌 ||	12
Lily	||	2

1 **Our Model Cars**

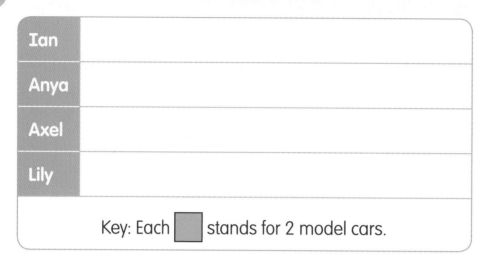

Ian	
Anya	
Axel	
Lily	

Key: Each ⬜ stands for 2 model cars.

2 **Our Model Cars**

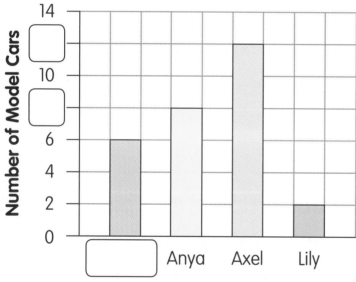

The scale on the bar graph has skips of _____.

INDEPENDENT PRACTICE

Use the picture graph to complete each bar graph.

The picture graph shows the number of each type of kite some students made after school.

Kites Made by the Students

Fish	🪁 🪁 🪁 🪁 🪁 🪁
Round	🪁 🪁 🪁 🪁
Butterfly	🪁 🪁 🪁 🪁 🪁 🪁
Bird	🪁 🪁 🪁 🪁 🪁 🪁 🪁 🪁

Key: Each 🪁 stands for 1 kite.

Abigail used the data from the picture graph to make a vertical and a horizontal bar graph. She used a scale of 2.

1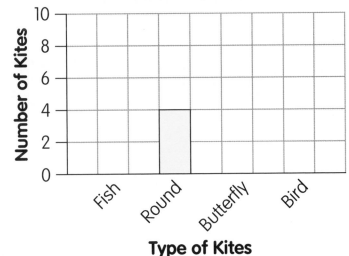

2

**Kites Made by
the Students**

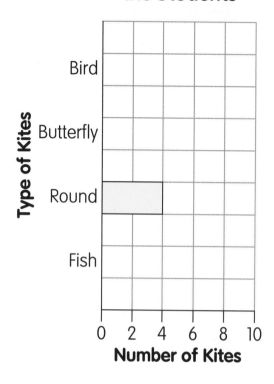

**Complete the tally chart and bar graph.
Then, answer each question.**

Brayden went to a bird park and saw five types of birds.
He recorded the number of each type of bird he saw in a tally chart.

3

Birds Brayden Saw at the Bird Park

Type of Birds	Tally	Number of Birds
Eagle	✚✚✚ ✚✚✚ ✚✚✚ ✚✚✚	
Ostrich		8
Parrot	‖‖‖	4
Peacock	✚✚✚ ✚✚✚ ✚✚✚ ‖	
Penguin		24

4

Birds Brayden Saw at the Bird Park

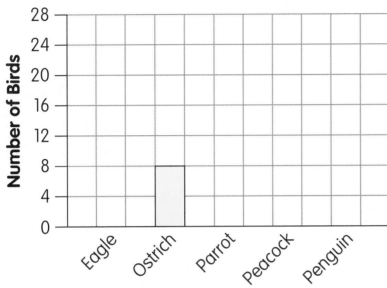

5 The scale shows skip counts of _____.

6 **Mathematical Habit 6** Use precise mathematical language

What is the greatest number on the vertical axis?
Explain.

_____

_____

_____

_____

_____

Count the number of each type of mask made.
Complete the tally chart and bar graph.
Then, fill in each blank.

Simone and her friends made some animal masks.

cat masks

sheep masks

rabbit masks

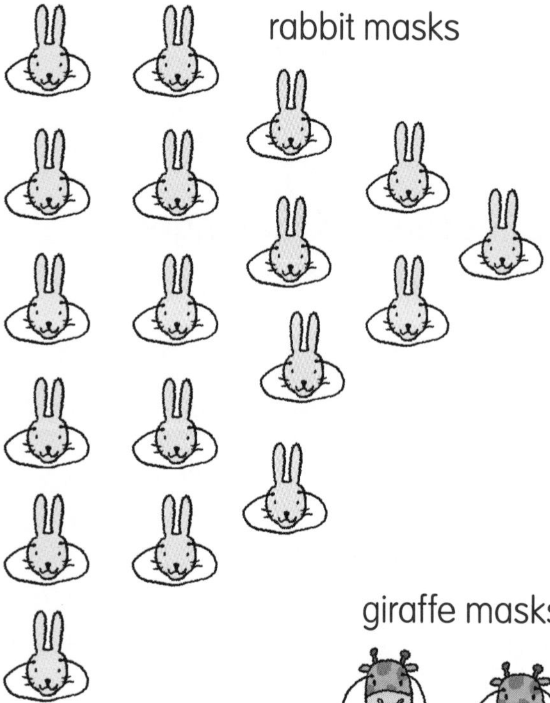

monkey masks

giraffe masks

7 **Masks Made by Simone and Her Friends**

Type of Masks	Tally	Number of Masks
Cat		
Sheep		
Monkey		
Rabbit		
Giraffe		

8 **Masks Made by Simone and Her Friends**

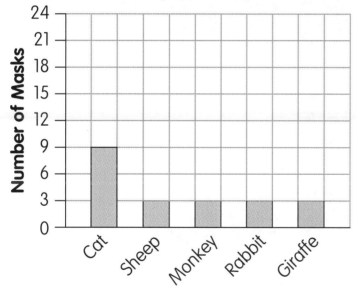

9 The scale shows skip counts of _____.

10 The greatest number on the scale is _____.

Complete each bar graph.
Then, fill in each blank.

The picture graph shows the number of points five players scored in a basketball game.

Points Scored by Five Players

Key: Each 🏀 stands for 5 points.

11

Points Scored by Five Players

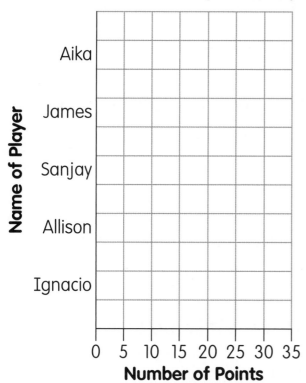

Name of Player

Aika

James

Sanjay

Allison

Ignacio

0   5   10   15   20   25   30   35

Number of Points

12

Points Scored by Five Players

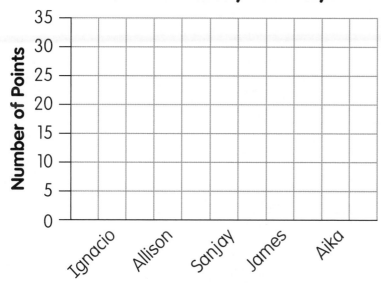

Number of Points

35
30
25
20
15
10
5
0

Ignacio   Allison   Sanjay   James   Aika

Name of Player

13 The scales show skip counts of _____.

14 The greatest number on each scale is _____.

A survey was carried out to find the favorite activities of third graders.

It was found that …

10 like to read books.

12 like to make crafts.

Twice as many children like to play sports as to make crafts.

4 fewer children like to visit friends than play sports.

Complete the bar graph and fill in the missing activity names.

15

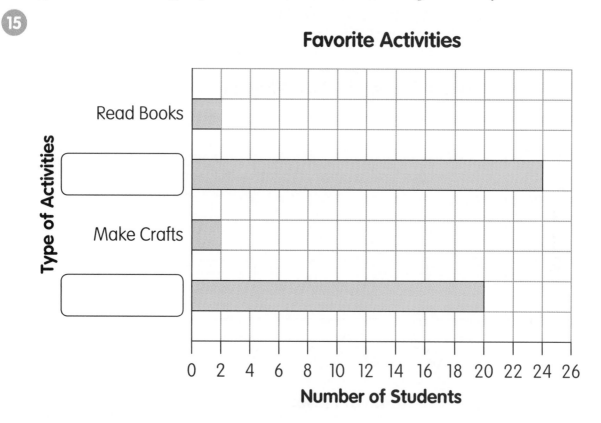

Favorite Activities

Name: _____   Date: _____

3 Reading and Interpreting Bar Graphs

Learning Objective:
• Read and interpret data from bar graphs with scales.

THINK

The table shows the number of colored balls in a box.
Draw a bar graph to represent the information.

Color	Red	Blue	Yellow	Green
Number of Balls	9	16	6	?

a   There are more green balls than red balls.
The number of green balls can be divided by 3.
How many green balls are there?

b   How many blue balls must be added
so that there are 60 balls in all?

ENGAGE

Roll a pair of  20 times.
Record the sum of each pair of results in the tally chart below.

Sum	2	3	4	5	6	7	8	9	10	11	12
Tally											

Draw a bar graph to display your results.
How did you do it? Discuss with your partner.

LEARN Solve problems using bar graphs

1 Sofia sold tickets from Monday to Friday last week. She drew a bar graph to show the number of tickets she sold each day.

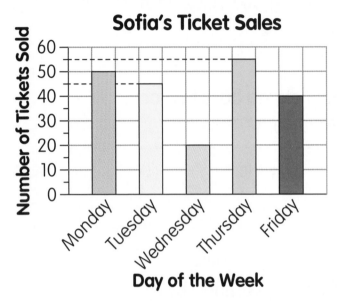

Sofia's Ticket Sales

a How many tickets did Sofia sell on Monday?

Sofia sold 50 tickets on Monday.

b On which day did Sofia sell 45 tickets?

45 lies exactly halfway between 40 and 50.

She sold 45 tickets on Tuesday.

c   On which day did she sell the least number of tickets?
    She sold the least number of tickets on Wednesday.

d   How many fewer tickets did she sell on
    Monday than on Thursday?

    55 tickets were sold on Thursday.
    50 tickets were sold on Monday.

    55 − 50 = 5

    She sold 5 fewer tickets on Monday than on Thursday.

e   On which day did she sell twice as many
    tickets as on another day?

40 tickets were sold on Friday.
20 tickets were sold on Wednesday.
40 is 20 two times.

She sold twice as many tickets on Friday as on Wednesday.

TRY Practice solving problems using bar graphs

Use the data in the bar graph to answer each question.

The bar graph shows the number of pages read in a day by Maite and her friends.

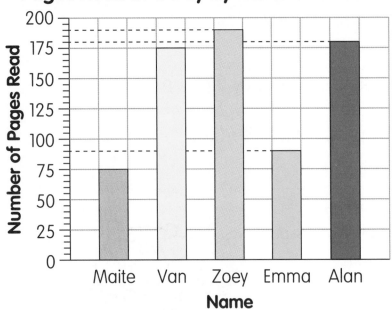

Pages Read in a Day by Maite and Her Friends

1. How many pages did Zoey read? _____

2. Who read 90 pages? _____

3. Who read the most pages? _____

4. Who read the fewest pages? _____

5 How many more pages did Zoey read than Maite? _____

6 Who read twice as many pages as Emma? _____

7 Alan wants to read twice as many pages as Van.

How many more pages must he read? _____

8 How many pages did Maite, Zoey, and Emma read in all? _____

Use the data in the bar graph to answer each question.

The bar graph shows the favorite colors of a group of children.

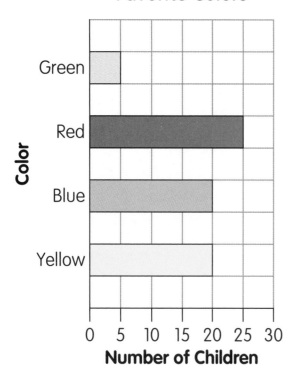

Favorite Colors

9. How many more children like yellow than green? _____

10. How many children like green and yellow? _____

11. 8 children who chose red were boys.

   How many girls chose red? _____

12. 10 children changed their mind and chose green instead of blue.

   How many children like green now? _____

Name: _____ Date: _____

Use the data in the bar graph to answer each question.
Write T for true and F for false in the boxes.

The bar graph shows the number of notebooks that five students have.

Notebooks that Five Students Collected

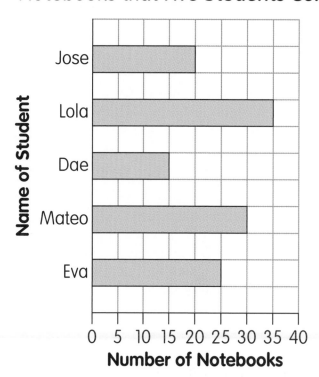

1 Jose has 20 notebooks.

2 Eva has 25 notebooks.

3 Lola has 40 notebooks.

4 Mateo has 5 fewer notebooks than Eva.

5 Dae has the least number of notebooks.

Use the data in the bar graph to answer each question.

The bar graph shows the bus tickets that were sold on Monday, Tuesday, Wednesday, and Thursday.

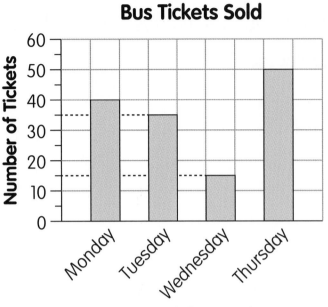

Bus Tickets Sold

6 How many more tickets were sold on Thursday than on Wednesday? _____

7 On Thursday, 15 of the tickets sold were for children. How many tickets sold were for adults? _____

8 18 fewer tickets were sold on Friday than on Tuesday. How many tickets were sold on Friday? _____

9 The number of tickets sold on Tuesday are grouped into fives. How many groups are there? _____

10 How many tickets were sold during the four days? _____

Use the data in the bar graph to answer each question.

The bar graph shows the number of badges five students collected.

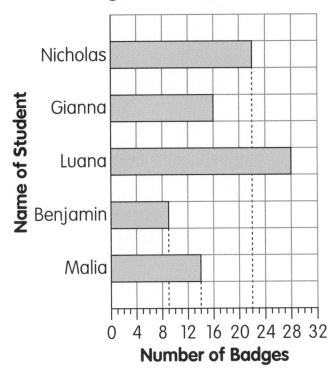

Badges Five Students Collected

Name of Student: Nicholas, Gianna, Luana, Benjamin, Malia

Number of Badges: 0 4 8 12 16 20 24 28 32

11 How many more badges did Malia collect than Benjamin?

_____

12 How many fewer badges did Gianna collect than Luana?

_____

13 How many badges did Gianna and Luana collect altogether?

_____

14 Who collected twice as many badges as Malia?

_____

15 Which two students collected a total of 31 badges?

_____

Use the data in the bar graph to answer each question.

The bar graph shows the kinds of juices that people like.

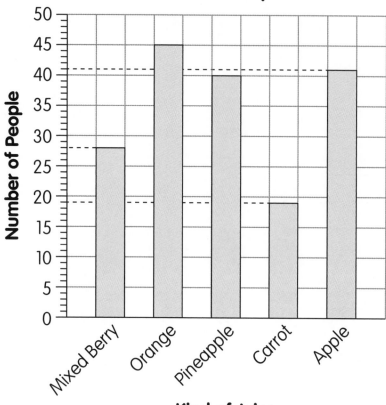

Juices that People Like

Number of People

Mixed Berry   Orange   Pineapple   Carrot   Apple

Kind of Juice

16 _____ people like mixed berry juice.

17 19 people like _____ juice.

18 The most popular juice is _____.

19 13 more people like apple juice than _____ juice.

20 5 fewer people like _____ juice than the most popular juice.

21 What can you say about orange juice and carrot juice?

_____

_____

Use the data in the bar graph to answer each question.

Jason sold flowers at the farmer's market.
The bar graph shows the number of flowers he sold.

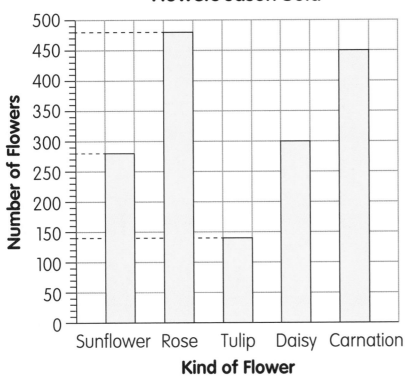

Flowers Jason Sold

22 How many daisies did Jason sell? _____

23 He sold 150 more carnations than another flower.

Which kind of flower is it? _____

24 He sold twice as many sunflowers as another kind of flower.

Which kind of flower is it? _____

25 How many fewer sunflowers than roses were sold? _____

26 He sold a total of 750 of two kinds of flowers.

Which two kinds of flowers could they be? _____

Use the data in the bar graph to answer each question.

The bar graph shows the subjects that a number of students like.

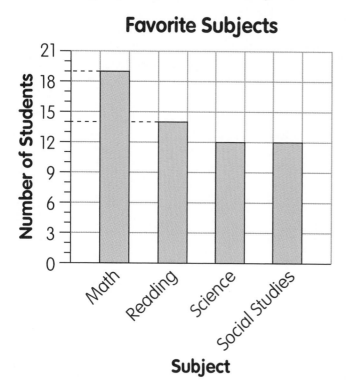

Favorite Subjects

27 _____ students like Math.

28 2 fewer students like _____ than reading.

29 The number of students who like _____ is equal to the number of students who like _____.

30 A total of 38 students like three different subjects. Which three subjects could they be?

_____

Line Plots and Estimation

Learning Objectives:
- Use a ruler to estimate and measure given lengths to the nearest quarter, half, or whole inch.
- Show data on a line plot where the horizontal scale is marked off in whole numbers, halves, or quarters.

THINK

Draw eight lines that are less than 3 inches.
Use an inch ruler to measure each line.
Then, draw a line plot to show the data.

ENGAGE

Draw two lines of the same length.
Make two equal intervals on the first line,
and four equal intervals on the second line.
Now, mark two points nearer to $\frac{1}{2}$ on the first line,

and two points nearer to $\frac{1}{4}$ on the second line.

LEARN Estimate and measure lengths to the nearest half or quarter inch

1 This is an inch ruler.

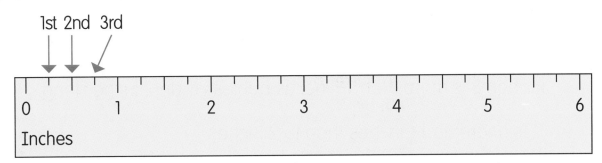

The first division marking on the ruler is the $\frac{1}{4}$-inch mark.

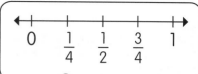

The second division marking is the $\frac{1}{2}$-inch mark.

The third division marking is the $\frac{3}{4}$-inch mark.

2 Sydney wants to estimate the lengths of two ribbons.

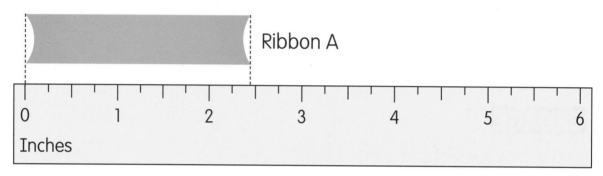

Ribbon A

Ribbon A is more than 2 inches but less than $2\frac{1}{2}$ inches long.

It is nearer to $2\frac{1}{2}$ inches than to 2 inches.

So, the length of Ribbon A is $2\frac{1}{2}$ inches to the nearest half inch.

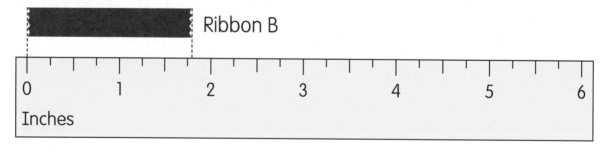

Ribbon B

Ribbon B is more than $1\frac{3}{4}$ inches but less than 2 inches long.

It is nearer to $1\frac{3}{4}$ inches than to 2 inches.

So, the length of Ribbon B is $1\frac{3}{4}$ inches to the nearest quarter inch.

Estimating and measuring lengths to the nearest half or quarter inch

Work in groups.

(1) Measure each line to the nearest half or quarter inch.

——————————————— A

——————————————— B

——————————— C

——————————————— D

——————— E

———————————————— F

————— G

——————————— H

———————————————— I

Measure each line using an inch ruler.

——————————— J

(2) Record your data in a tally chart.

Measured Length (in.)	Tally	Line
1		
$1\frac{1}{4}$		
$1\frac{1}{2}$		
$1\frac{3}{4}$		
2		
$2\frac{1}{4}$		
$2\frac{1}{2}$		
$2\frac{3}{4}$		
3		

(3) Then, show your data on the line plot.

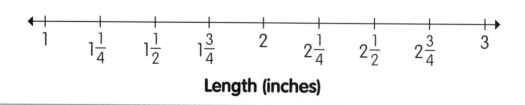

Length (inches)

TRY Practice estimating and measuring lengths to the nearest half or quarter inch

Measure the line to the nearest half inch.
Fill in each blank.

1

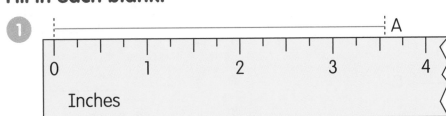

Line A is more than _____ inches but less than _____ inches.

It is nearer to _____ inches than to _____ inches.

Line A is _____ inches to the nearest half inch.

Measure the line to the nearest quarter inch.
Fill in each blank.

2

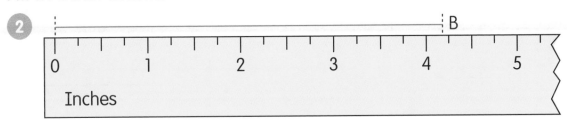

Line B is more than _____ inches but less than _____ inches.

It is nearer to _____ inches than to _____ inches.

Line B is _____ inches to the nearest quarter inch.

Measure each line to the nearest half or quarter inch. Then, show your data on the line plot.

3 ——————————— A   _____ in.

4 —————— B   _____ in.

5 ——————————— C   _____ in.

6 ————————————————— D   _____ in.

7 ———————————————————— E   _____ in.

8 ———————————————————— F   _____ in.

9 ———————————————————————————— G   _____ in.

10 ——————————————————————————————— H   _____ in.

11 ——————————————————————————— I   _____ in.

12 ——————————————————————— J   _____ in.

13 ————————————————————————————————— K   _____ in.

14 ——————————————————————————— L   _____ in.

15

Length (inches)

Name: _____ Date: _____

INDEPENDENT PRACTICE

**Estimate the length of each line without using a ruler.
Then, measure each line to the nearest quarter inch.**

1 ———————————————— A Estimated length: _____ in.

Measured Length: _____ in.

2 ——————————— B Estimated length: _____ in.

Measured Length: _____ in.

**Measure the length of each rope.
Then, check (✔) each correct statement.**

Rope C

Rope D

Rope E

3 Rope C is more than $2\frac{1}{2}$ inches but less than 3 inches long. ☐

4 Rope C is 3 inches long to the nearest half inch. ☐

5 Rope C is $2\frac{1}{2}$ inches long to the nearest half inch. ☐

6 Rope D is $2\frac{3}{4}$ inches long to the nearest quarter inch. ☐

7 Rope D is $2\frac{1}{2}$ inches long to the nearest half inch. ☐

8 Rope E is more than $1\frac{1}{4}$ inches but less than $1\frac{1}{2}$ inches long. ☐

9 Rope E is $1\frac{1}{4}$ inches long to the nearest quarter inch. ☐

10 Rope E is $1\frac{1}{2}$ inches long to the nearest half inch. ☐

Measure each line to the nearest half inch. Then, complete the line plot.

11 ————————————— H   _____ in.

12 ———————————— I   _____ in.

13 ——— J   _____ in.

14 ———————————————— K   _____ in.

15 ————————————————— L   _____ in.

16 —————————————————— M   _____ in.

17 ——————————————————— N   _____ in.

18 ———————————————————— P   _____ in.

19 ————————————————————— Q   _____ in.

20 ————————————————————— R   _____ in.

21 ———————————————————————— S   _____ in.

22 ——————————————————————— T   _____ in.

23

Length (inches)

1 Mathematical Habit 5 Use tools strategically

Measure each line to the nearest half or quarter inch. Record each measurement in the table below.

_____ A   _____ B

___ C   _____ D

_____ E   _____ F

_____ G   _____ H

_____ J   _____ K

Line	A	B	C	D	E
Length					

Line	F	G	H	J	K
Length					

Use the data in the table to make a line plot.
Follow the steps to help you.

STEP 1 Draw a number line that has all the measurements required. Label the measurements and give your line plot a title.

STEP 2 Make an ✗ representing each line above its measurement.

STEP 3 Check that the number of ✗s shows the data in the table.

2 **Mathematical Habit** **2** **Use mathematical reasoning**

Use the data in the line plot to answer each question.

a How did you get the least and greatest number on the number line?

_____

_____

_____

b Imagine you had to show the measurements of 100 lines. Would a line plot be a good way to show the data? Explain.

_____

_____

_____

Problem Solving with Heuristics

Mathematical Habit 1 Persevere in solving problems

Mr. Miller recorded the growth of his tree over five months.
He drew a picture graph and a bar graph to show the data.

Growth of Mr. Miller's Tree over Five Months

January	🌱🌱🌱🌱🌱🌱🌱🌱🌱🌱🌱🌱🌱🌱🌱🌱🌱🌱
February	🌱🌱🌱🌱🌱🌱🌱🌱🌱🌱
March	🌱🌱🌱🌱🌱🌱🌱🌱🌱🌱🌱
April	🌱🌱🌱🌱🌱🌱🌱🌱
May	🌱🌱🌱🌱🌱🌱

Key: Each 🌱 stands for 2 centimeters.

1 Use the information in the picture graph to fill in the table.

Month	January	February	March	April	May
Growth of tree					

2 Complete the bar graph.

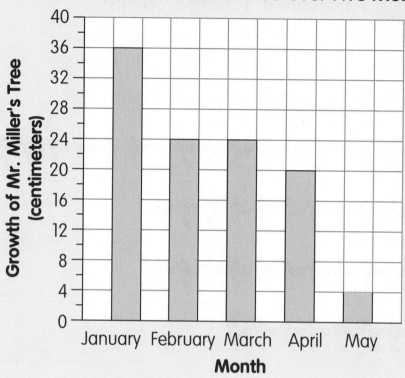

Growth of Mr. Miller's Tree over Five Months

3 In which month(s) did his tree grow by 24 centimeters?

4 For which month was the bar graph incorrectly drawn?

5 How much more did his tree grow in February than in May?

6 His tree was 30 centimeters tall before January.
What was the height of his tree at the end of May?

CHAPTER WRAP-UP

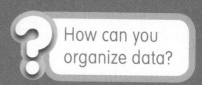
Bar Graphs and Line Plots

Tally Chart

A tally chart is used to record and organize data. A tally mark on the chart stands for 1 of something.

Our Model Cars

Name	Tally	Number of Model Cars
Ian	ⵜⵜ	6
Anya	‖‖	3
Axel	ⵜⵜ ‖‖‖	9
Lily	‖‖	3

Bar Graph

A bar graph uses bars to show data. The scales show the value of the bars.

Favorite Fruit

Favorite Fruit	Apple	Peach	Orange	Pear
Number of Children	10	15	25	20

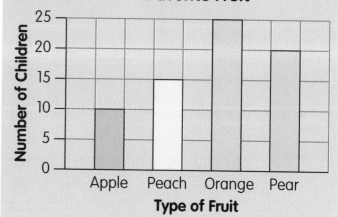

Favorite Fruit

Line Plots

A line plot is used to show data.

Line	P	Q	R	S	T	U
Length	$1\frac{3}{4}$ in.	1 in.	$1\frac{1}{4}$ in.	$1\frac{1}{2}$ in.	$1\frac{1}{4}$ in.	$1\frac{3}{4}$ in.

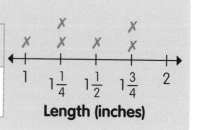

Name: _____ Date: _____

Use the data in the picture graph to answer each question.

The picture graph shows the types of food that a
group of children had for breakfast.

Type of Breakfast Food

	Bun	◯◯◯◯◯
	Pancake	◯◯◯◯
	Sandwich	◯◯◯◯◯◯◯◯◯
	Cereal	◯◯◯◯◯◯
	Muffin	

Key: Each ◯ stands for 5 children.

1 Twice as many children had muffins as pancakes for breakfast.
   Complete the picture graph.

2 _____ children had buns for breakfast.

3 45 children had _____ for breakfast.

4 The greatest number of children had _____ for breakfast.

5. The least number of children had _____ for breakfast.

6. _____ more children had muffins than buns for breakfast.

7. _____ children were surveyed in all.

Complete the tally chart and bar graph.
Then, answer each question.

Constance took a walk in a park and saw 5 types of insects.
She recorded the number of each type of insect she saw in a tally chart.

8.

Insects Seen at the Park

Type of Insects	Tally	Number of Insects
Ant	卌 卌 卌 卌 卌 卌 卌 卌 ‖	
Bee	卌 卌 卌 卌 卌	
Beetle	卌 卌 卌 卌 卌 ‖‖	
Butterfly		33
Dragonfly		25

9

Insects Seen at the Park

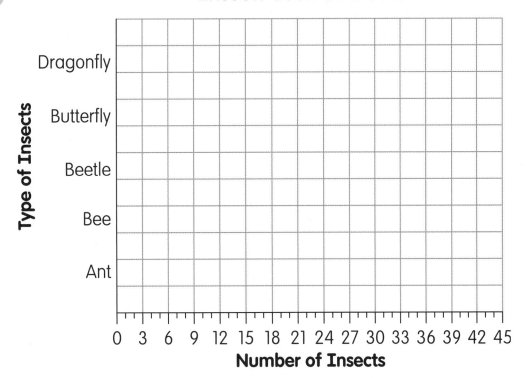

10 Constance saw the greatest number of _____ at the park.

11 She saw the same number of _____ and _____.

12 She saw 9 more _____ than butterflies.

13 She saw a total of _____ butterflies and beetles.

14 She saw _____ insects in all.

Measure each line to the nearest half or quarter inch.
Record your answers in the tally chart.
Then, complete the line plot.

15 ——————————————— A   _____ in.

16 ——————————— B   _____ in.

17 ——————————— C   _____ in.

18 ——————————— D   _____ in.

19 ——————————— E   _____ in.

20 ——————————— F   _____ in.

21 ——————————— G   _____ in.

22 ————————————————— H   _____ in.

23 ————————— J   _____ in.

24 ——————————— K   _____ in.

25

Length of Lines

Length	Tally	Number of Lines
1 in.		
$1\frac{1}{4}$ in.		
$1\frac{1}{2}$ in.		
$1\frac{3}{4}$ in.		
2 in.		
$2\frac{1}{4}$ in.		
$2\frac{1}{2}$ in.		
$2\frac{3}{4}$ in.		
3 in.		

26

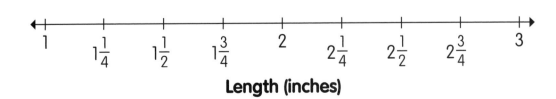

Length (inches)

Assessment Prep

Answer each question.

27 Paige's mother gave her a sticker for every 2 books read each day. She put them on a picture graph as shown below. The stickers for the books read on Monday were not put on the graph.

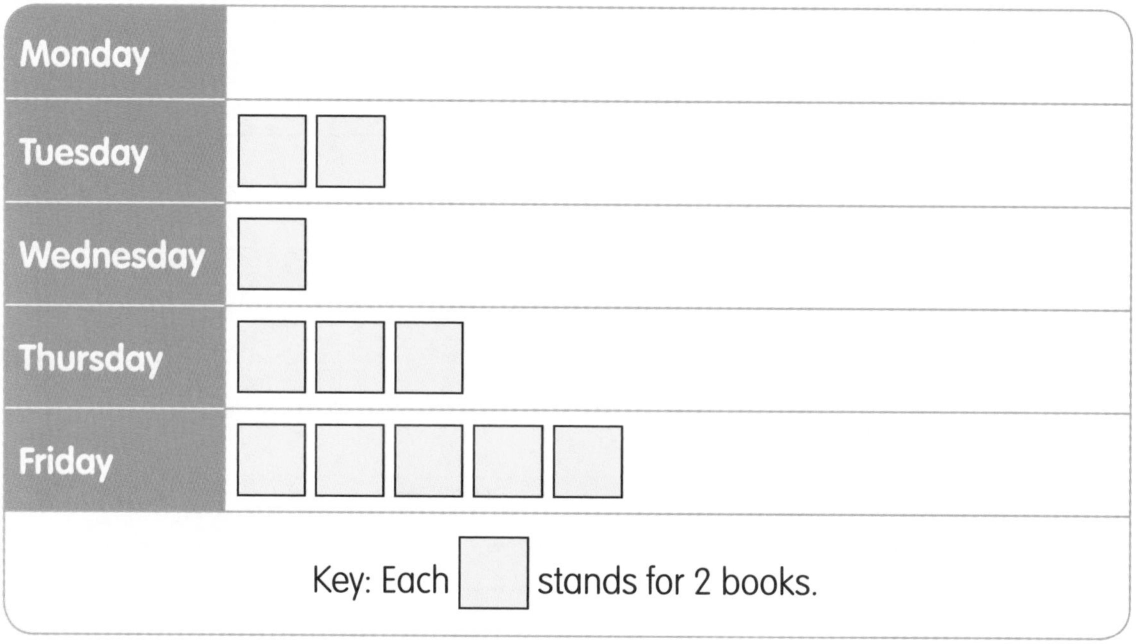

Monday	
Tuesday	☐ ☐
Wednesday	☐
Thursday	☐ ☐ ☐
Friday	☐ ☐ ☐ ☐ ☐

Key: Each ☐ stands for 2 books.

Use the data in the picture graph to answer the question.
Paige read 36 books in all during the five days.
How many books did Paige read on Monday?

(A) 7

(B) 12

(C) 14

(D) 25

28 The bar graph shows the number of points four children scored in a quiz.

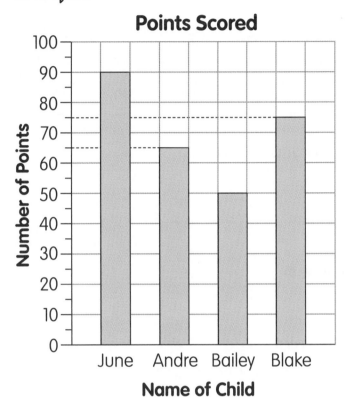

Points Scored

Use the data in the bar graph to answer the question.
Who scored more than 70 points?
Choose the **two** correct answers.

(A) June

(B) Andre

(C) Bailey

(D) Blake

29 Rodrigo measures the length of 8 pieces of ribbons with a ruler. The results are shown in the table.

Ribbon	A	B	C	D	E	F	G	H
Length	$3\frac{1}{2}$ in.	5 in.	4 in.	$2\frac{3}{4}$ in.	$3\frac{1}{2}$ in.	$4\frac{1}{4}$ in.	$3\frac{3}{4}$ in.	$4\frac{1}{2}$ in.

Then, Rodrigo made a line plot of the data.

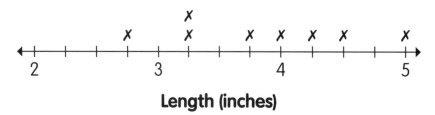

Length (inches)

Explain Rodrigo's mistake.
What should the correct line plot be?
Write your explanation and answer in the space below.

Name: _____   Date: _____

Waiting at a Bus Stop

Elizabeth and Eduardo were at a bus stop.
They waited 10 minutes for their bus to arrive.
While waiting, Elizabeth saw 5 types of vehicles passing by.
Eduardo measured the length of some twigs near the bus stop.

1 Elizabeth recorded the number of each vehicle that passed in a tally chart.

a Complete the tally chart.

Vehicles Passing By

Type of Vehicles	Tally	Number of Vehicles
Bus	|||| |||| |||| ||||	
Taxi	|||| |||| |||| |||| |||| |||| ||	
Car	|||| |||| |||| |||| |||| |||| |||| |||| |||| |||	
Motorcycle		10
Truck	||||		

b Use the data in the tally chart to complete the bar graph.

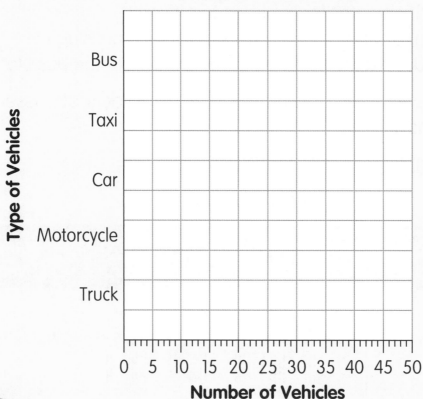

Vehicles Passing By

Type of Vehicles

Bus

Taxi

Car

Motorcycle

Truck

0   5   10   15   20   25   30   35   40   45   50

Number of Vehicles

BUS STOP

c   How many taxis passed by during the 10-minute period?
    How many fewer motorcycles than taxis passed by?

d   Twice as many buses as another vehicle passed by during the
    10-minute period. Which type of vehicle was that?

2 Eduardo measured the length of each twig to the nearest quarter or half inch. He recorded the data in the table and line plot.

Twig	Length
A	$3\frac{1}{4}$ in.
B	4 in.
C	$1\frac{3}{4}$ in.
D	$3\frac{1}{4}$ in.
E	$2\frac{3}{4}$ in.
F	$3\frac{1}{4}$ in.
G	$3\frac{1}{2}$ in.
H	$2\frac{1}{2}$ in.

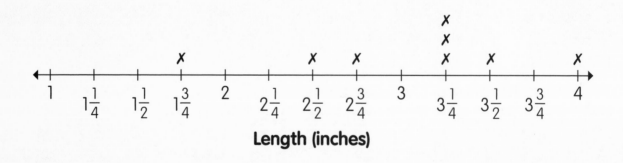

Length (inches)

a   How many twigs are longer than 3 inches?

b   What is the most common length of the twigs measured?

Rubric

Point(s)	Level	My Performance
7–8	4	• Most of my answers are correct. • I showed complete understanding of what I have learned. • I used the correct strategies to solve the problems. • I explained my answers and mathematical thinking clearly and completely.
5–6.5	3	• Some of my answers are correct. • I showed some understanding of what I have learned. • I used some correct strategies to solve the problems. • I explained my answers and mathematical thinking clearly.
3–4.5	2	• A few of my answers are correct. • I showed little understanding of what I have learned. • I used a few correct strategies to solve the problems. • I explained some of my answers and mathematical thinking clearly.
0–2.5	1	• A few of my answers are correct. • I showed little or no understanding of what I have learned. • I used a few strategies to solve the problems. • I did not explain my answers and mathematical thinking clearly.

Teacher's Comments

Chapter 12
Angles, Lines, and Two-Dimensional Figures

How can you classify polygons?

Name: _____ Date: _____

Identifying lines and curves

These are lines.

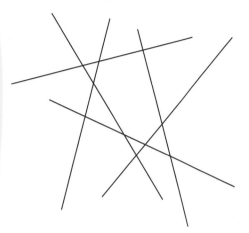

These are curves.

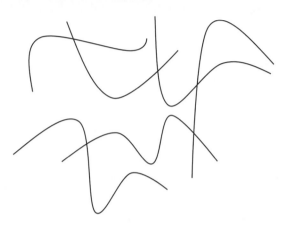

These figures are made with lines.

    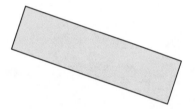

These figures are made with lines and curves.

 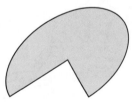  

▶ Quick Check

Circle each line.
Make an X on each curve.

Circle each figure that is made with lines only.
Make an X on each figure that is made with line(s)
and curve(s).

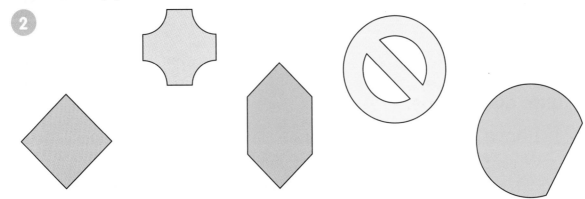

Chapter 12 Angles, Lines, and Two-Dimensional Figures **339**

Counting the number of sides and corners of flat shapes

Plane Shape	Number of Sides	Number of Corners
circle	0	0
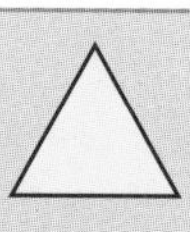 triangle	3	3
square	4	4
 rectangle	4	4
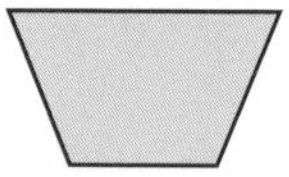 trapezoid	4	4
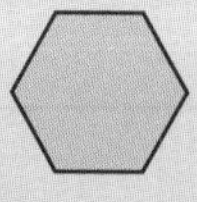 hexagon	6	6

▶ **Quick Check**

Name each shape.

③ I have 3 sides and 3 corners.
What shape am I?

_____

④ I have 6 sides and 6 corners.
What shape am I?

_____

Combining flat shapes to form other flat shapes

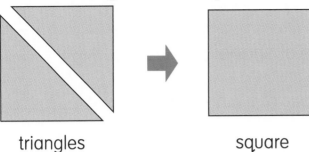

triangles   square

Two triangles can be combined to form a square.

▶ **Quick Check**

Circle the shape you get when you combine two **.**

Circle each set that makes **.**

Use some △ **to make two different flat shapes.**
Draw the shape formed.
Then, fill in each blank.

7

Name of shape: _____

Number of triangles used: _____

⑧

Name of shape: _____

Number of triangles used: _____

Separating flat shapes into smaller flat shapes

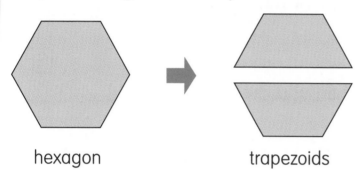

hexagon → trapezoids

A hexagon can be separated into two trapezoids.

▶ **Quick Check**

Draw a line to separate the rectangle into smaller flat shapes in two different ways. Then, fill in each blank.

⑨

Name of shapes: _____

Number of smaller shapes: _____

⑩

Name of shapes: _____

Number of smaller shapes: _____

Drawing shapes on dot paper and grid paper

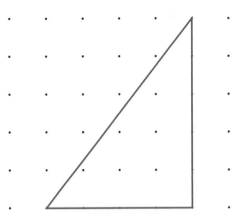

dot paper

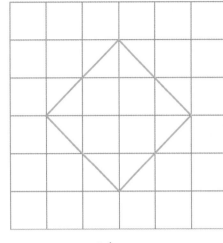

grid paper

▶ **Quick Check**

Copy each shape on the dot paper or grid paper.
Name each shape drawn.

11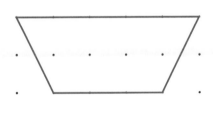

Name of shape: _____

12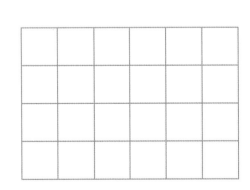

Name of shape: _____

Identifying angles in shapes

In a shape, two sides meet at a point to form an angle.

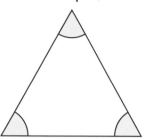

The triangle has three angles.

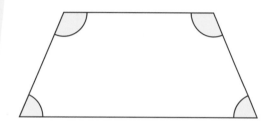

The trapezoid has four angles.

▶ **Quick Check**

Mark all the angles in each shape.

13

14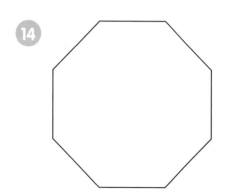

1 Introducing Angles

Learning Objectives:
- Find angles in plane figures and real-world objects.
- Compare angles to a right angle.

New Vocabulary
point   line
line segment   endpoint
right angle

THINK

Draw separate diagrams by joining

a   three dots,   b   four dots,   c   five dots.

In each diagram, join any two dots to form a line segment in as many ways as possible.
Write down the number of line segments and the number of angles formed. What pattern do you see?
How many line segments and angles can be formed with 6 dots?
Draw a diagram to show your answer.

ENGAGE

a   Draw three dots.
    Connect the dots to form a flat shape.
    What shape is it?

b   Now, draw four dots.
    Connect the dots to form a flat shape.
    What shape is it?
    Show a different way to draw the shape.

LEARN Identify and name a point, line, and line segment

1   A point is an exact location in space.

A

You can write this point as Point A.

A line is a straight path.
It goes on without end in both directions.

This line passes through Points *A* and *B*.
You can write it as Line *AB* or Line *BA*.

A line segment is part of a line.
It has two endpoints.

This line segment has two endpoints, *C* and *D*.
You can write it as Line segment *CD* or Line segment *DC*.

Hands-on Activity **Identifying and naming a point, line,
and line segment**

① Draw three points in the space below.
Label the points *P*, *Q*, and *R*.

② Join the points to form three line segments.
Name the three line segments.

The three line segments are _____, _____, and _____.

TRY Practice identifying and naming a point, line, and line segment

Identify each figure as a **point, line,** or **line segment.**

1 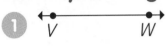 V   W

_____

2 • X

_____

3  Y

Z

_____

Find the number of line segments that make up each shape.

4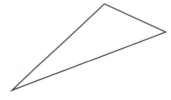

_____

5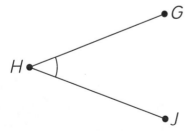

_____

ENGAGE

Draw two line segments on a grid to make an angle.
What do you notice? Is it true that any two lines can make an angle?
Explain the different types of angles you can draw.

LEARN Identify an angle

1 When two line segments share the same endpoint, they form an angle.

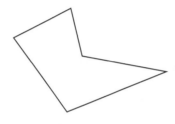

• G

H •

• J

Draw a curve to mark the angle.

This angle is formed by two line segments, *HG* and *HJ*.
The line segments have the same endpoint *H*.

You can make an angle with your arm.

2 Look at the square and triangle.

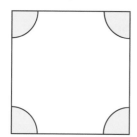

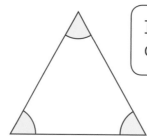

In a flat shape, two sides meet at a point to form an angle.

The square has four angles.
The triangle has three angles.

3 Angles can also be found on objects with flat shapes.

In an object, two sides meet at a corner to form an angle.

How many angles can you find around you?

Hands-on Activity Identifying an angle

Work in pairs.

1. Draw a 3-sided, 4-sided, 5-sided, and 6-sided shape below.

2. Mark and color each angle in the shape.

3. Complete the table to show the number of angles in each shape.

Shape	3-sided	4-sided	5-sided	6-sided
Number of Angles				

TRY Practice identifying an angle

Look at each pair of  and answer each question.

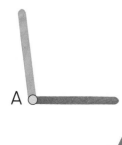

A

B

C

D

E

F

1 Which pairs form an angle? _____

2 Which pairs do not form an angle? _____

Check (✓) each pair of line segments that form an angle.
Make an X on each pair of line segments that do not form an angle.

3

A _____ B

D

C

☐

4
E

G

F H

☐

5
P

Q

R

☐

6
W

Y   Z

X

☐

Find the number of angles in each flat shape.

 7

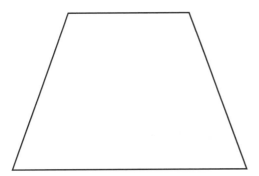

_____

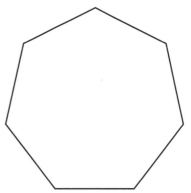 **8**

_____

A flat shape is outlined on each object.
Find the number of angles in each flat shape.

 9

_____

10

_____

11

_____

12

_____

Fill in each blank with fan, box, or scissors.

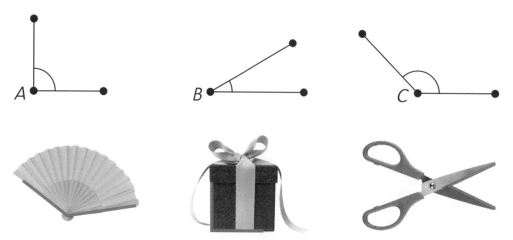

13 Angle *A* is about the same size as the angle on the _____.

14 Angle *B* is about the same size as the angle on the _____.

15 Angle *C* is about the same size as the angle on the _____.

ENGAGE

Draw a square, a triangle, and a trapezoid.
Mark the angles in each flat shape.
What do you notice about the size of each angle?
Describe in writing the different types of angles you see.

LEARN Compare other angles to a right angle

1 Fold a sheet of paper twice to make an angle like this:

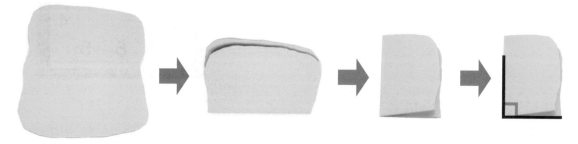

The corner of the folded paper is a right angle.

You can use the folded paper to check for a right angle and mark it as shown.

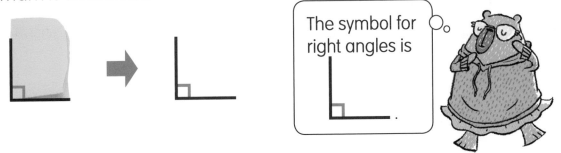

The symbol for right angles is ⌐.

The  can be used to find right angles in objects like these.

You can use 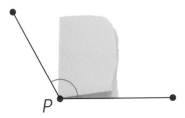 to check the angles in a square.

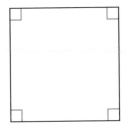

There are four right angles in a square.

You can also use the  to check if angles are greater than or less than a right angle.

P

Q

Angle P is greater than a right angle.

Angle Q is less than a right angle.

Hands-on Activity

Activity 1   Making angles

① Your teacher will provide you with a set of paper strips labeled 1 and 2.

② Paste Strip 2 on the space below.

③ Fasten Strip 1 onto Strip 2 so that only Strip 1 moves.

④ Turn Strip 1 to form a right angle.
Draw and mark the angle formed.

Example:

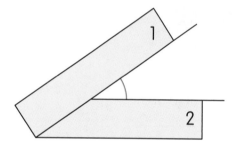

5 Repeat ① to ④ to make the following angles.

   a an angle less than a right angle

   b an angle greater than a right angle

   c an angle which is about twice the size of a right angle

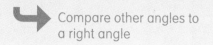

Activity 2   Comparing other angles to a right angle

Work in groups of three.

(1) Use a ⬜ to find right angles, and angles less than or greater than a right angle in objects around the school.

(2) Take photos of the objects and print them out.
Paste the photos on the space below.

(3) Use a red marker to mark the angles on the objects.

(4) Describe the angles to your group members.

TRY Practice comparing other angles to a right angle

Compare each angle to a 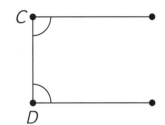 **.**
Then, answer each question.

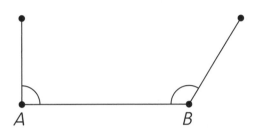 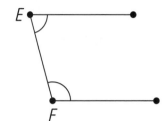

1. Which angles are the same size as right angles?

   _____

2. Which angles are greater than right angles?

   _____

3. Which angle is less than a right angle?

   _____

Compare each angle to a ⌐ **.**
Write less than, greater than, or equal to in each blank.

4.   This angle is _____ a right angle.

5.    This angle is _____ a right angle.

6.    This angle is _____ a right angle.

Use a 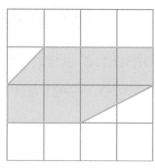 to find the number of right angles in each shape.

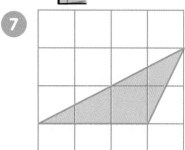

7

_____

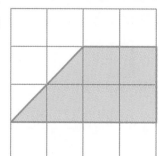

8

_____

9

_____

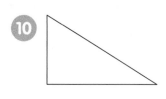

10

_____

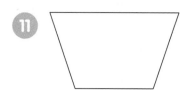

11

_____

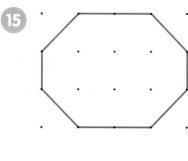

12

_____

Use a 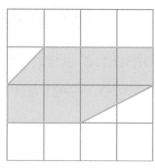 to find the number of angles less than a right angle in each shape.

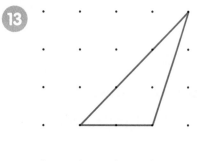

13

_____

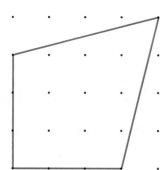

14

_____

15

_____

Draw the shape on the grid.

16 Draw a four-sided shape with one angle greater than a right angle and one angle less than a right angle.

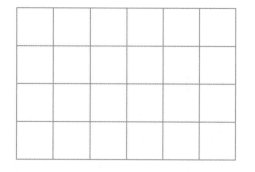

Name: _____ Date: _____

INDEPENDENT PRACTICE

Check (✓) the statements that correctly describe each figure.

1

• A

☐ This is a point.

☐ It represents any location in space.

☐ It represents an exact location in space.

☐ It cannot be found in space.

2

B
C

☐ This is a line.

☐ This is a line segment.

☐ It is a straight path.

☐ It has two endpoints.

☐ It goes on without end in both directions.

3

D
E

☐ This is a line.

☐ This is a line segment.

☐ It is part of a line.

☐ It is a straight path.

☐ It has two endpoints.

☐ It goes on without end in both directions.

Identify each figure as a point, line, or line segment. Name each figure.

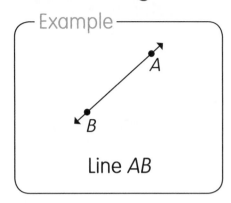

Example

Line *AB*

4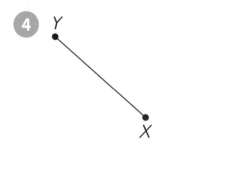

_____

5

_____

6 •
T

_____

Check (✓) the box if an angle is shown. Then, mark the angle.

7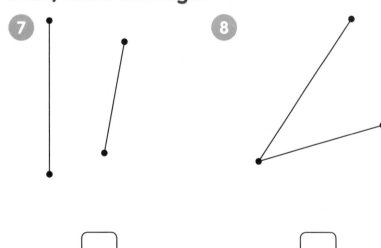

8

9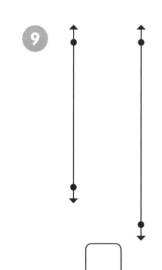

☐   ☐   ☐

10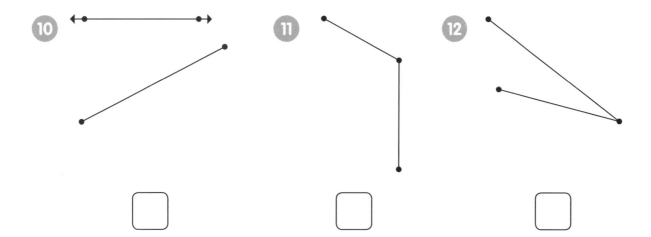

☐

11

☐

12

☐

Mark two angles on each object.

13

14

15

16

17

18

Compare each angle to a [ ].

Check (✓) the statement that correctly describes each angle.

⑲	[ ] This angle is a right angle.
	[ ] This angle is greater than a right angle.
	[ ] This angle is less than a right angle.
⑳	[ ] This angle is a right angle.
	[ ] This angle is greater than a right angle.
	[ ] This angle is less than a right angle.
㉑	[ ] This angle is a right angle.
	[ ] This angle is greater than a right angle.
	[ ] This angle is less than a right angle.

Mark all the right angles in each figure.

㉒

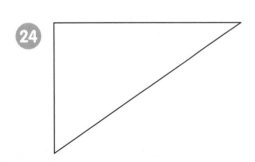

㉓

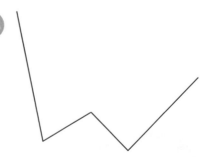

㉔

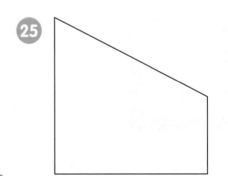

㉕

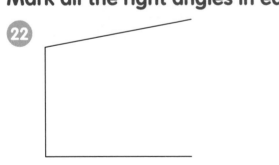

2 Introducing Perpendicular and Parallel Lines

Learning Objectives:
- Define and identify perpendicular lines.
- Define and identify parallel lines.

New Vocabulary
perpendicular   parallel

THINK

Take four . Show your partner how you can make

a   2 pairs of perpendicular lines with three craft sticks.

b   3 pairs of perpendicular lines with four craft sticks.

In each part, how many pairs of parallel lines did you make?

ENGAGE

a   Make as many pairs of line segments that form right angles on a 🔲. Show your partner where the different right angles are.

b   Look around the classroom to identify right angles.

LEARN Identify perpendicular lines

1 Look at the lines drawn on the grid.

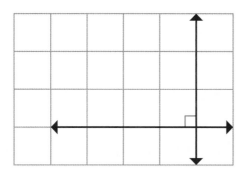

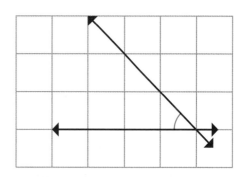

These two lines meet at right angles.

They are perpendicular lines.

These two lines do not meet at right angles.

They are not perpendicular lines.

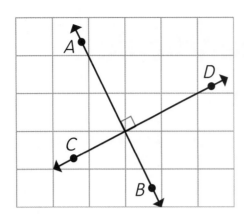

Lines *AB* and *CD* meet at right angles.
Line *AB* is perpendicular to Line *CD*.

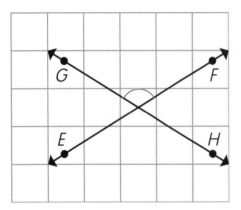

Lines *EF* and *GH* do not meet at right angles.
Line *EF* is not perpendicular to Line *GH*.

2 How can you check whether two lines are perpendicular?

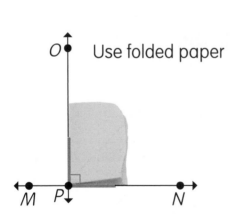

Use folded paper

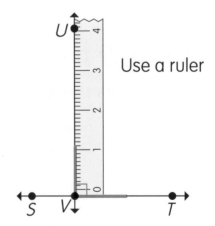

Use a ruler

Put the folded paper against the two lines as shown.
The lines meet at a right angle.
So, Line *OP* is perpendicular to Line *MN*.

Put a ruler against the two lines as shown.
The lines meet at a right angle.
So, Line *UV* is perpendicular to Line *ST*.

③ You can find perpendicular line segments in objects like these.

  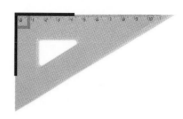

Hands-on Activity Identifying perpendicular line segments

Work in groups of four.

① Look around your school.
Find objects with perpendicular line segments and objects with no perpendicular line segments.

② Use a ruler to check if the line segments are perpendicular.

③ Complete the tables below.

Objects with Perpendicular Line Segments	Places Where I Found the Objects
bench	hallway

Objects with no Perpendicular Line Segments	Places Where I Found the Objects
tree branch	schoolyard

TRY Practice identifying perpendicular lines

Check (✓) the box below each pair of perpendicular lines.

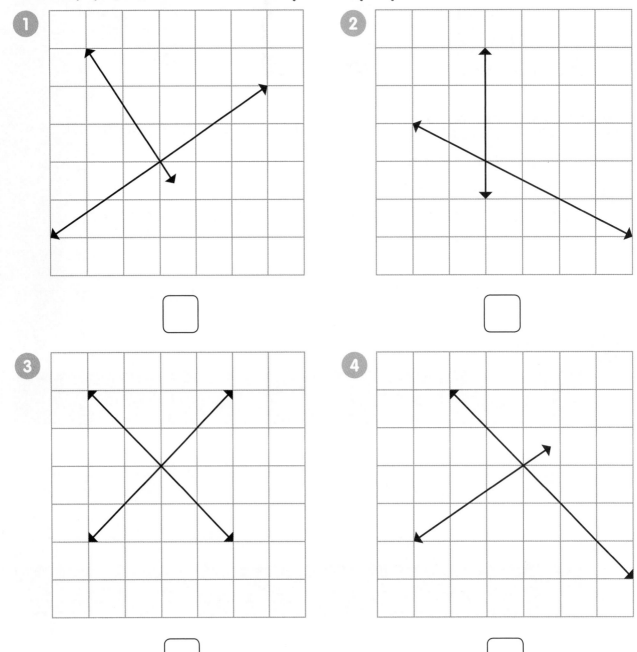

Name the perpendicular line segments in each figure.

5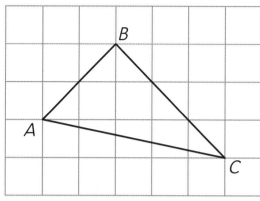

_____

6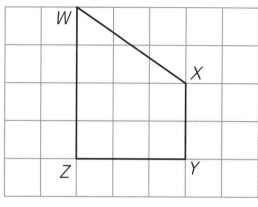

_____

_____

Answer each question.

7 Which line is perpendicular to Line *AB*?

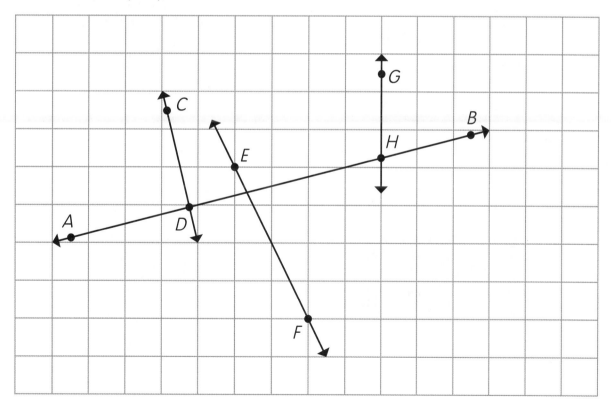

Line _____ is perpendicular to Line *AB*.

8 How many pairs of perpendicular line segments can you find on the square face of the box below?

I can find _____ pairs of perpendicular line segments.

Name two pairs of perpendicular line segments on each object.

9 A _____ B

D _____ C

_____

_____

_____

10 E _____ F

H _____ G

_____

_____

_____

11 J _____ K

M _____ L

_____

_____

_____

12 P _____ Q

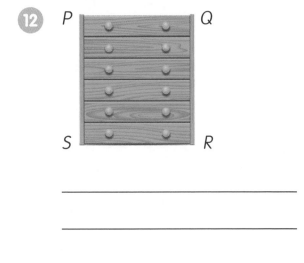

S _____ R

_____

_____

_____

ENGAGE

Is it possible to draw two lines that will never meet?
How do you know?
Draw a sketch to show your explanation.
What are some real-world examples of lines that never meet?
Explain.

LEARN Identify parallel lines

1 Look at the lines drawn on the grid.

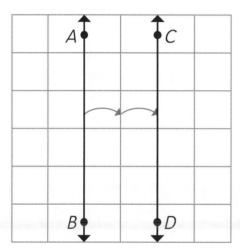

Lines *AB* and *CD* are two lines that will not meet no matter how long you draw them.

The distance between them is always the same.

> The two lines are always 2 units apart.

They are parallel lines.

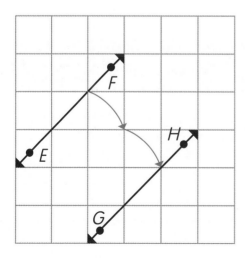

Lines *EF* and *GH* are parallel.
Line *EF* is parallel to Line *GH*.

2 You can find parallel line segments in objects like these.

Hands-on Activity Identifying parallel line segments

Work in groups of four.

1 Look around your school.
Find objects with parallel line segments and objects with no parallel line segments.

2 Complete the table below.

Objects with Parallel Line Segments	Places Where I Found the Objects
tabletop	classroom

Objects with no Parallel Line Segments	Places Where I Found the Objects
leaf	schoolyard

TRY Practice identifying parallel lines

Check (✓) the box below each pair of parallel lines.

1

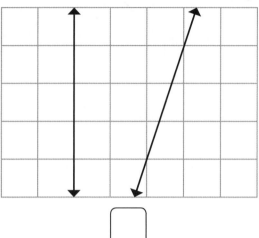

▢

2

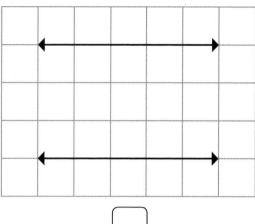

▢

3

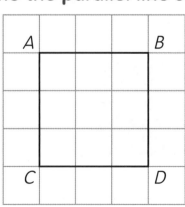

▢

4

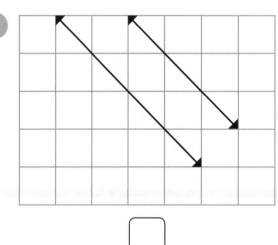

▢

Name the parallel line segments in each figure.

5

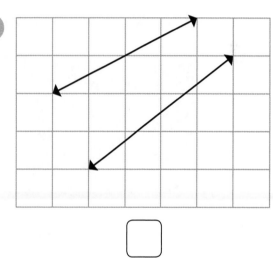

_____

_____

6

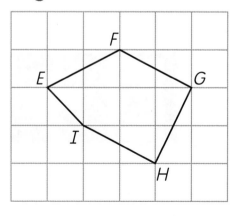

_____

_____

7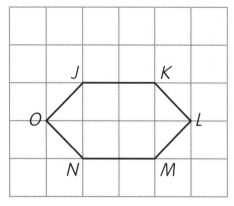

_____

_____

_____

8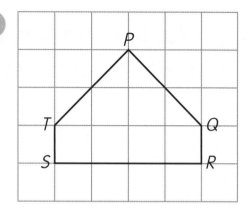

_____

_____

_____

Name the two pairs of parallel line segments on each object.

9

_____

_____

_____

10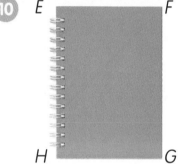

_____

_____

_____

11

_____

_____

_____

12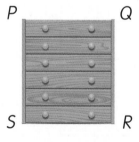

_____

_____

_____

Name: _____ Date: _____

INDEPENDENT PRACTICE

Check (✓) the box beside each pair of perpendicular lines.

1 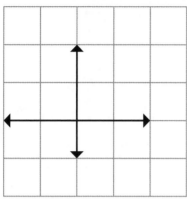 ☐

2 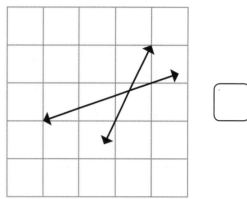 ☐

3 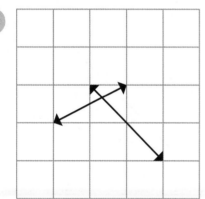 ☐

4 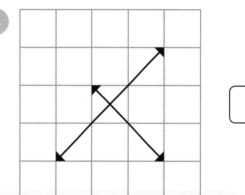 ☐

5 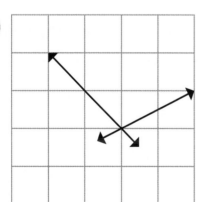 ☐

6 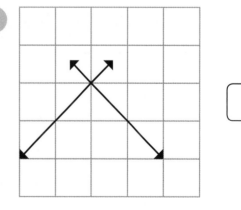 ☐

Circle the pair of perpendicular lines in each figure.

7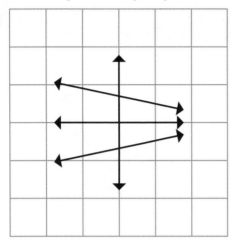

8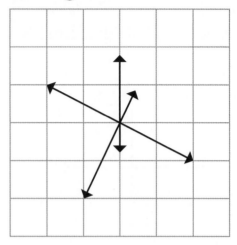

9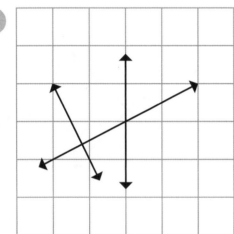

10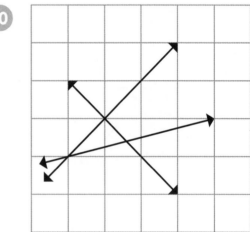

Circle each letter that has a pair of perpendicular line segments.

11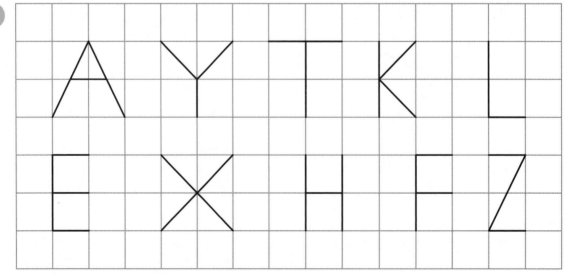

Name all the pairs of perpendicular line segments in each figure.

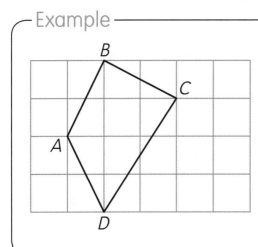

Line segments *AB* and *BC*

12

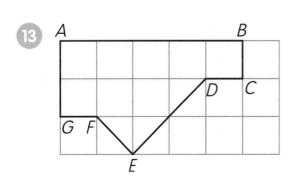

_____

_____

13

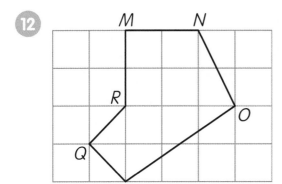

_____

_____

_____

_____

_____

14

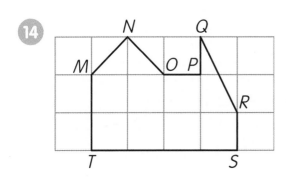

_____

_____

_____

_____

Check (✓) the box beside each pair of parallel lines.

15 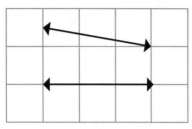 ☐

16 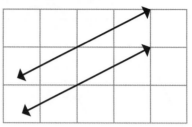 ☐

17 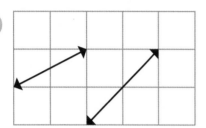 ☐

18 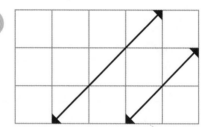 ☐

19 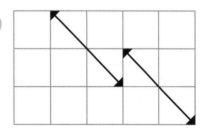 ☐

20 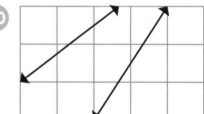 ☐

Circle the pair of parallel lines in each figure.

21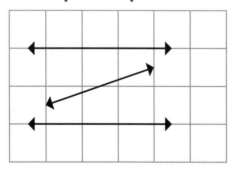

22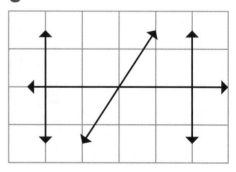

23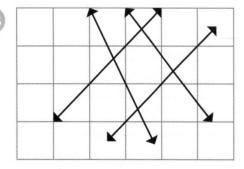

24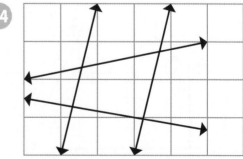

Circle each letter that has a pair of parallel line segments.

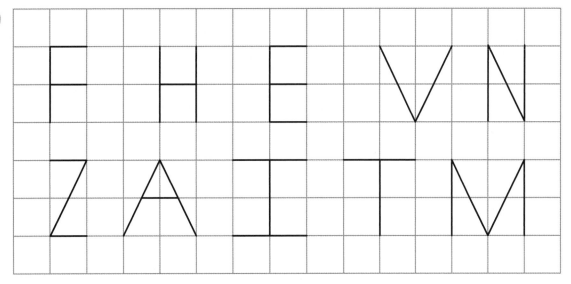

Name all the pairs of parallel line segments in each figure.

┌─ Example ──┐

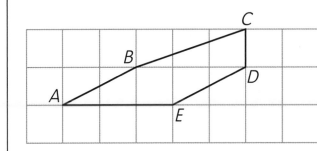

Line segments *AB* and *ED*

└──┘

26

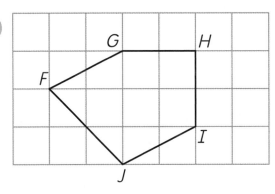

_____

27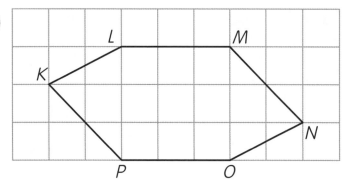

_____

_____

_____

28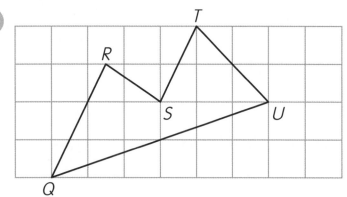

_____

Name a pair of perpendicular line segments and a pair of parallel line segments in each figure.

29

Perpendicular line segments: _____

Parallel line segments: _____

30

Perpendicular line segments: _____

Parallel line segments: _____

3 Polygons

Learning Objectives:
- Identify open and closed plane figures.
- Identify and describe special polygons.
- Identify and describe special quadrilaterals.
- Recognize polygons by their attributes.

New Vocabulary
open plane figure
closed plane figure
plane figure
polygon
vertex
parallelogram
rhombus

THINK

The solid is formed using a cuboid and a square-based pyramid.
Look at the solid from different directions.
Which of the following are not possible figures you would see?

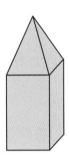

a   b   c   d   e

ENGAGE

Draw three figures that start and end at the same point.
Share your drawings with your partner.

You can use lines and curves to draw figures.

LEARN Identify open and closed plane figures

1

Group A

The figures in Group A do not start and end at the same point. They are open plane figures.

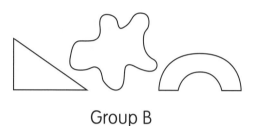

Group B

The figures in Group B start and end at the same point. They are closed plane figures.

Plane figures are flat figures. They may be open or closed.

TRY Practice identifying open and closed plane figures

Identify each figure as an open or a closed plane figure. Circle each correct answer.

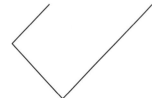

open / closed

open / closed

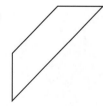

open / closed

open / closed

Complete the table. Write yes or no.

5

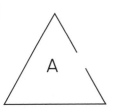
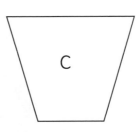
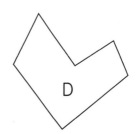

Property	A	B	C	D
It is a closed plane figure.				
There are 3 or more line segments.				

ENGAGE

The figure on the right is made up of different shapes. Label each shape with a letter and write its name.

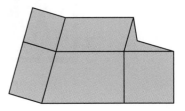

LEARN Identify polygons

1 Closed plane figures can be put into two groups.

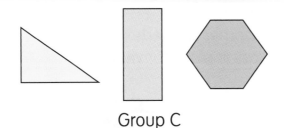

Group C

The figures in Group C are formed using line segments only.
They are called polygons.

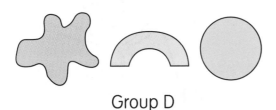

Group D

The figures in Group D are not formed using line segments only.
They are not polygons.

> A polygon is a closed plane figure formed using three or more line segments.

> Two line segments cannot meet to form a closed figure. So, two line segments cannot form a polygon.

2 Polygons can be classified according to the number of sides they have.

These are some polygons and their names.

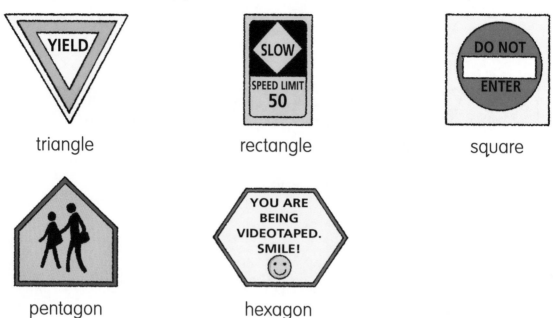

triangle   rectangle   square

pentagon   hexagon

In a polygon, each line segment is called a side.
Two sides of a polygon meet at a point called the vertex.
An angle is formed when the two sides meet at the vertex.

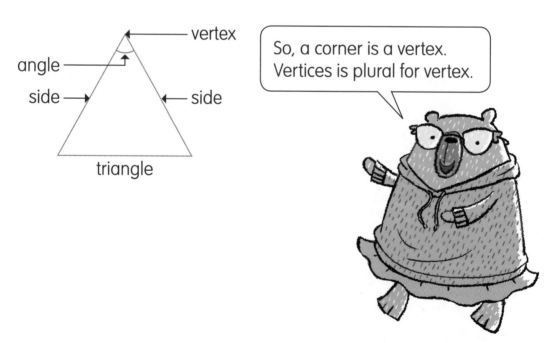

vertex

angle

side   →   ←   side

triangle

So, a corner is a vertex.
Vertices is plural for vertex.

Work in pairs.

Activity 1   Identifying polygons

(1) Use two ▓ to form a figure.
Draw your figure in the space below.

(2) Use five ▓ to form a closed figure and an open figure.
Draw your figures below.

(3) Use six ▓ to form a closed figure and an open figure.
Draw your figures below.

(4) Discuss with your partner which of your figures are polygons.
Name the polygons.

Activity 2 Identifying special polygons

(1) Draw four polygons in the space below.
Each polygon should have a different number of sides.

(2) Name your polygons and fill in the table.

Name of Polygons	Number of Sides	Number of Angles	Number of Vertices

(3) **Mathematical Habit 6** Use precise mathematical language

What do you notice about the number of sides, angles, and vertices of a polygon?

TRY Practice identifying polygons

Circle each polygon.

1

A

B

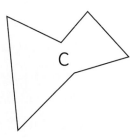

C

D

E

F

Mark each angle in the pentagon.
Fill in the name of each part of the pentagon.
Then, complete the table.

2

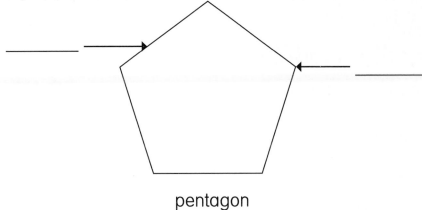

_____ →   ← _____

pentagon

3

Number of Sides	Number of Angles	Number of Vertices

Write true or false for each statement.

4 A hexagon has seven vertices and six sides. _____

5 A square and a rectangle have four vertices and four angles each. _____

6 All polygons have four sides. _____

Answer the question.

7 I am a polygon.
I have 1 more vertex than a square.
What am I? _____

ENGAGE

How many different polygons can you draw using exactly four line segments? Make a sketch of each polygon and share it with your partner.

LEARN Identify quadrilaterals

1 These are quadrilaterals.

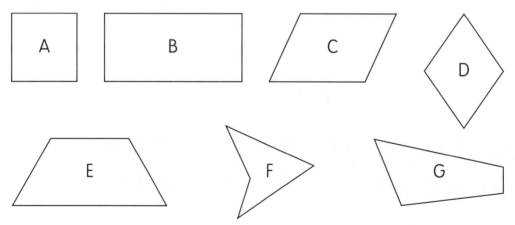

A quadrilateral is a polygon with 4 sides and 4 angles.

2 You can find quadrilaterals in objects around you.

3 Some quadrilaterals have special names.
They are classified by

a the pairs of sides that are parallel.

b the number of sides that are of equal lengths.

c the number of right angles.

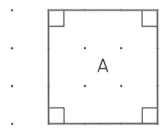

Figure A is a square.
Opposite sides of a square are parallel.
All sides of a square are of equal length.
All four angles of a square are
right angles.

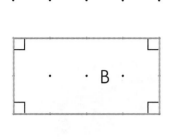

Figure B is a rectangle.
Opposite sides of a rectangle are parallel.
Only the opposite sides of a rectangle are of equal length.
All four angles of a rectangle are right angles.

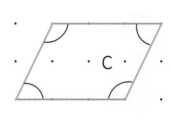

Figure C is a parallelogram.
Opposite sides of a parallelogram are parallel.
Only the opposite sides of a parallelogram are of equal length.
There are four angles in a parallelogram.

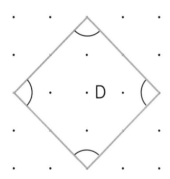

Figure D is a rhombus.
Opposite sides of a rhombus are parallel.
All sides of a rhombus are of equal length.
There are four angles in a rhombus.

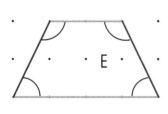 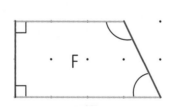

Figures E and F are trapezoids.
Only one pair of opposite sides are parallel.
There are four angles in a trapezoid.

A trapezoid can have two right angles.

Work in pairs.

1. Make five quadrilaterals with special names on a .
   Draw them in the grid below.

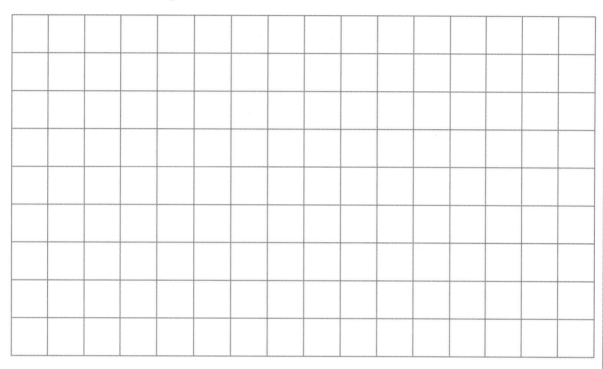

2. Name the quadrilaterals you have drawn.

_____

3. **Mathematical Habit 6** Use precise mathematical language

   Explain how the quadrilaterals are the same or different.

_____

_____

_____

_____

_____

TRY Practice identifying quadrilaterals

Circle each quadrilateral.

 1

Write true or false for each statement.

2 The outline of a dollar bill is a quadrilateral. _____

3 The outline of a bottle cap is a quadrilateral. _____

4 The outline of an envelope is a quadrilateral. _____

5 The outline of a penny is a quadrilateral. _____

Fill in each blank.

6

A rectangle has _____ pair(s) of parallel sides,

_____ pair(s) of sides that are of equal length,

and _____ right angle(s).

7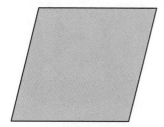

A rhombus has _____ pair(s) of parallel sides,

_____ sides that are of equal length, and

_____ angle(s).

8

A trapezoid has _____ pair(s) of parallel sides

and _____ angles.

A trapezoid can have _____ right angle(s).

9

A parallelogram has _____ pair(s) of parallel sides,

_____ pair(s) of sides that are of equal length,

and _____ angle(s).

FLASH CARDS!

What you need:

Players: 2

Materials: Flash cards

What to do:

1 Player 1 holds the deck of cards.
He or she flashes the top card at Player 2.

2 Player 2 gives the special name of the figure on the card.
He or she gets 1 point if the answer is correct.
Player 1 flashes the next card at Player 2.

3 The game continues until one minute is up.
Players take turns to play.

Who is the winner?

The player who gets the most points in one minute wins.

Name: _____   Date: _____

INDEPENDENT PRACTICE

Check (✓) each box that shows the correct answer.

1

Figure	Statement	True	False
	It is a closed plane figure.		
	It is a polygon.		

2

Figure	Statement	True	False
	It is a closed plane figure.		
	It is a polygon.		

3

Figure	Statement	True	False
	It is a closed plane figure.		
	It is a polygon.		

4

Figure	Statement	True	False
	It is a closed plane figure.		
	It is a polygon.		

Complete the table below.

	Figure	Name	Number of Sides	Number of Angles	Number of Vertices
5					
6					
7					
8					
9					
10					

Circle the correct answer for each question.

11 A polygon with four sides is a quadrilateral / triangle / hexagon.

12 A quadrilateral with four sides of equal length and four right angles is a rectangle / square / rhombus.

13 A rectangle / square / rhombus is a quadrilateral that has two pairs of parallel sides, two pairs of sides that are of equal length, and four right angles.

14 A parallelogram / trapezoid / triangle is a quadrilateral with two pairs of parallel sides that are also of equal length.

15 A quadrilateral with all sides of equal length but no right angles is a rhombus / trapezoid / pentagon.

16 A rhombus / trapezoid / square is a quadrilateral with two sides that are parallel but not of equal length.

Draw each quadrilateral in the grid.

17 A parallelogram

18 A square

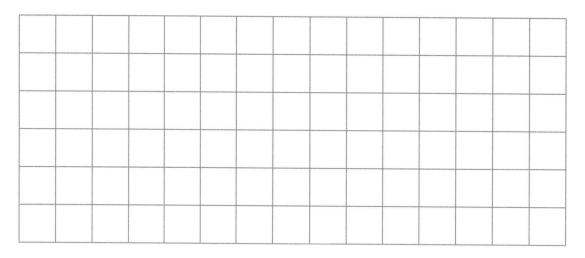

19 A trapezoid

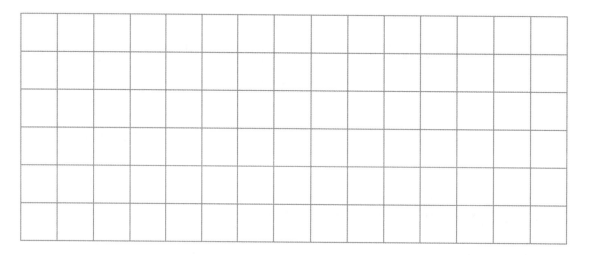

20 A quadrilateral that does not have a special name.

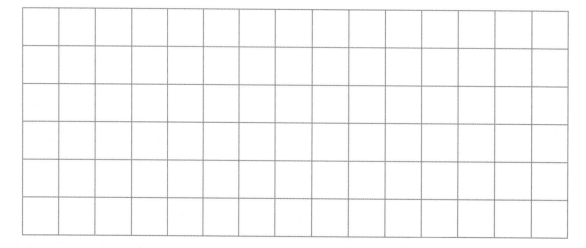

Name: _____   Date: _____

Mathematical Habit 6 Use precise mathematical language

1 Your classmate was absent from class when your teacher taught about perpendicular and parallel lines.

Write a letter to him explaining the difference between the lines.

_____

_____

_____

2 Explain why these figures are not polygons.

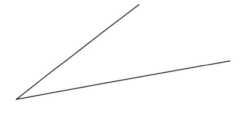

A

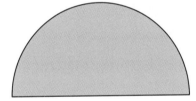

B

_____

_____

_____

3 I am a 4-sided polygon.
All my sides are equal.
What shape can I be? Explain.

_____

_____

_____

Problem Solving with Heuristics

1 **Mathematical Habit 6** Use precise mathematical language

Draw each shape on the dot paper.
Then, answer each question.

a A triangle with a right angle.

Can you draw a triangle with 2 right angles? _____

b A quadrilateral with 4 sides and 2 right angles only.

What do you notice about the other angles in the quadrilateral?

2 **Mathematical Habit 8** **Look for patterns**

Look at the pattern below.
These are the first five shapes in the pattern.

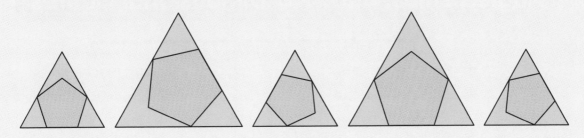

a Check (✔) the box that shows the next shape.

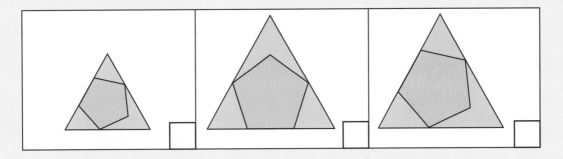

b Check (✔) the box that shows the eighth shape.

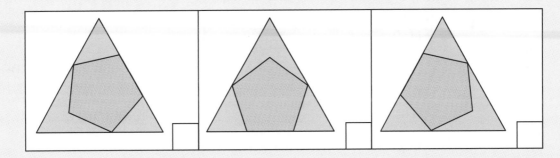

CHAPTER WRAP-UP

How can you classify polygons?

Angles, Lines, and Two-Dimensional Figures

Angles and Lines

Point:

A

Line:

A   B

Line segment:

C   D

Angles:

Right angle   Less than a right angle   Greater than a right angle

Polygons

A polygon is a closed flat figure formed by three or more line segments. Polygons have vertices, sides, and angles.

Examples:

Triangle △   Quadrilateral ▢
Pentagon ⬠   Hexagon ⬡

Special Quadrilaterals

Square ▢   Rectangle ▢
Rhombus ▱   Trapezoid ◺
Parallelogram ▱

Perpendicular and Parallel Lines and Segments

Perpendicular lines meet at right angles.
Parallel lines will not meet no matter how long you draw them.
The distance between them is always the same.

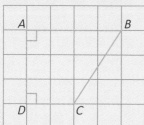

Perpendicular line segments:
Line segments AB and AD
Line segments AD and DC

Parallel line segments:
Line segments AB and DC

Name: _____ Date: _____

Answer the question.

1) Mark each angle in the figure.

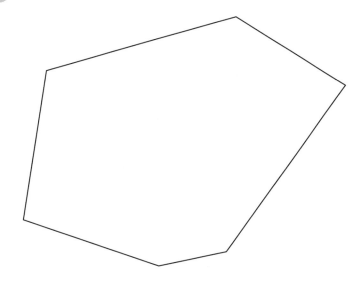

Compare each angle to a right angle.
Write less than, greater than, or equal to in each blank.

2)

This angle is _____ a right angle.

3)

This angle is _____ a right angle.

4)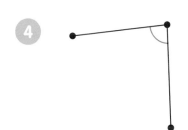

This angle is _____ a right angle.

Answer the question.

5 Name all the pairs of perpendicular line segments and parallel line segments in the figure below.

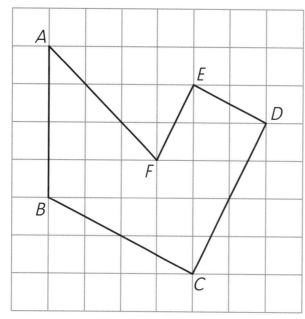

Perpendicular line segments:

_____

_____

_____

Parallel line segments:

_____

_____

Identify each figure as an open or a closed plane figure. Write open or closed.

6

This is a/an _____ plane figure.

7

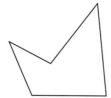

This is a/an _____ plane figure.

8

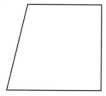

This is a/an _____ plane figure.

Complete the table below by drawing each polygon.

9			
Triangle	Hexagon	Quadrilateral	Pentagon

Name each quadrilateral.

10 _____

11 _____

12 _____

13 _____

14 _____

Write true or false for each statement.

15 The outline of a postcard is a quadrilateral. _____

16 The outline of a star is a quadrilateral. _____

17 A rhombus has 4 sides of equal length and
4 right angles. _____

18 A trapezoid has 1 pair of parallel sides and 4 angles. _____

19 A parallelogram has 2 pairs of parallel sides that are
of equal length and 4 right angles. _____

Assessment Prep

Answer each question.

20 Which **two** polygons are quadrilaterals?

(A)   (B)

(C)   (D)

21 I am a polygon with two pairs of parallel sides
and four right angles.
My opposite sides are of equal length.
What shape am I?   _____

22 Mackenzie drew three polygons and labeled them X, Y, and Z.
Figure X has twice as many sides as Figure Y.
Figure Z has 1 more side than a parallelogram.
Draw how the three polygons could look like in the grid below.
Name the polygons she drew.

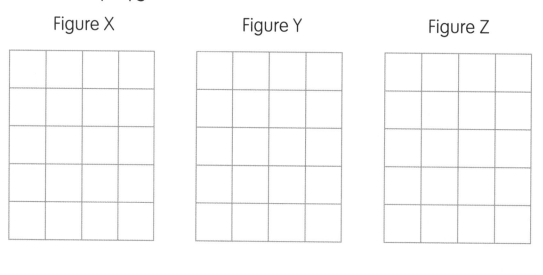

Figure X   Figure Y   Figure Z

_____   _____   _____

Name: _____ Date: _____

PERFORMANCE TASK

Building a Stadium

Mr. Allen is designing a stadium for the town.
He drew two designs for the community to vote for their favorite.

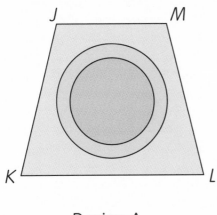

Design A

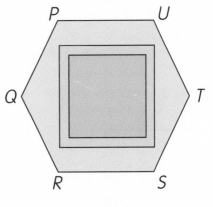

Design B

1 How many angles are there in the outline of each design?

Chapter 12 Angles, Lines, and Two-Dimensional Figures **405**

2 Are there any perpendicular line segments or parallel line segments in Design A? If there are, name them.

3 The outline of each design is a polygon. What is name of each polygon? Explain.

Rubric

Point(s)	Level	My Performance
7–8	4	• Most of my answers are correct. • I showed complete understanding of what I have learned. • I used the correct strategies to solve the problems. • I explained my answers and mathematical thinking clearly and completely.
5–6	3	• Some of my answers are correct. • I showed some understanding of what I have learned. • I used some correct strategies to solve the problems. • I explained my answers and mathematical thinking clearly.
3–4	2	• A few of my answers are correct. • I showed little understanding of what I have learned. • I used a few correct strategies to solve the problems. • I explained some of my answers and mathematical thinking clearly.
0–2	1	• A few of my answers are correct. • I showed little or no understanding of what I have learned. • I used a few strategies to solve the problems. • I did not explain my answers and mathematical thinking clearly.

Teacher's Comments

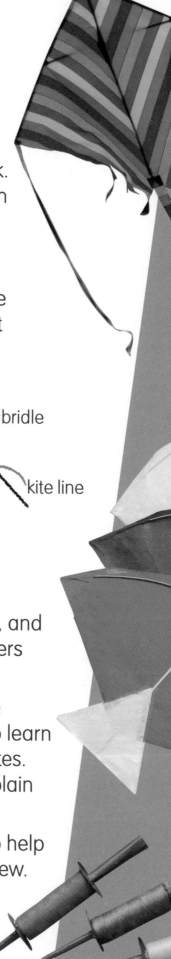

Forces on Kites

For centuries, inventors, scientists, and engineers have used kites in their work. The Wright brothers studied them when building their first airplane.

There are four forces that act on things that fly, including kites. These forces are lift, weight, drag, and thrust. They must be balanced to keep a kite flying.

Task

Make a Kite
Work in groups.

kite sail — bridle
cross spar —
spine —
kite line
tail

1 Draw a kite like the one on the right on a large piece of paper. Label the parts of the kite.

2 Count the number of sides, angles, and vertices in the kite. Write the numbers next to your drawing.

3 Go to the library or go online to the National Air and Space Museum to learn about the four forces that act on kites. Use your drawing to show and explain the forces.

4 Use books or search the internet to help you make a kite like the one you drew. Work with your teacher to plan a fly-a-kite day.

Chapter 12 Angles, Lines, and Two-Dimensional Figures

Glossary

A

- **area**

  Area is the amount of surface covered by a figure.
  It is measured in square units like square centimeters (cm^2), square inches (in^2), square meters (m^2), and square feet (ft^2).

  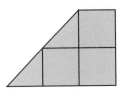

  The area of this figure is 4 square units.

C

- **capacity**

  Capacity is the greatest amount of liquid a container can hold.

  The capacity of the bottle is 600 milliliters.
  It now contains 350 milliliters of juice.

- **closed plane figure**

  Flat figures that start and end at the same point are called closed plane figures.

  Group B

D

- **denominator**

  The denominator is the number below the line of each fraction. It shows the number of equal part(s) the whole is divided into.

  $\frac{1}{2}$ ⟶ denominator

E

- **elapsed time**

  Elapsed time is the amount of time that has passed between the start and the end of an activity.

  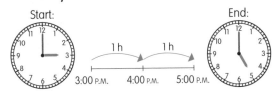

endpoint

Endpoint is the end of a line segment.

equivalent fractions

Equivalent fractions are two or more fractions that name the same parts of a whole.

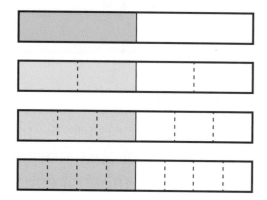

$\frac{1}{2}$, $\frac{2}{4}$, $\frac{3}{6}$, and $\frac{4}{8}$ are equivalent fractions.

F

fraction

A fraction is a number that names equal parts of a whole.

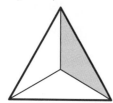

$\frac{1}{3}$ of the shape is shaded.

H

hour (h)

Hour (h) is a unit of measure for time.

1 h = 60 min
There are 60 minutes in 1 hour.

L

like fractions

Fractions with the same denominator are called like fractions.

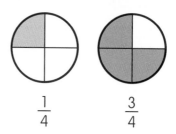

$\frac{1}{4}$ $\frac{3}{4}$

$\frac{1}{4}$ and $\frac{3}{4}$ are like fractions.

line

A line is a straight path. It goes on without end in both directions.

This line passes through Points A and B.
It can be called Line AB or Line BA.

line segment

A line segment is part of a line. It has two endpoints.

The endpoints of this line segment are Points C and D. It can be called Line segment CD or Line segment DC.

liter (L)

Liter (L) is a unit of measure for volume and capacity. It is used to measure large volumes.

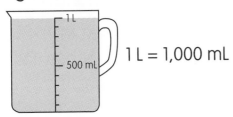

1 L = 1,000 mL

This measuring cup contains 1 liter of water.

M

milliliter (mL)

Milliliter (mL) is a unit of measure for volume and capacity. It is used to measure small volumes.

1,000 mL = 1L

This measuring cup contains 400 milliliters of water.

minute (min)

Minute (min) is a unit of measure for time.

1 minute

60 min = 1 h
There are 60 minutes in 1 hour.

N

numerator

The numerator is number above the line of each fraction. It shows the number of shaded part(s).

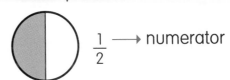

$\frac{1}{2}$ ⟶ numerator

O

open plane figure

Flat figures that do not start and end at the same point are called open plane figures.

Group A

P

parallel

Parallel lines do not meet no matter how long you draw them.
The distance between them is always the same.

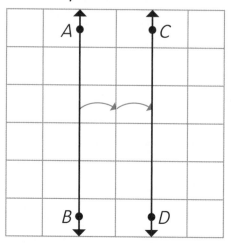

Line *AB* is parallel to Line *CD*.

parallelogram

A parallelogram is a quadrilateral. The opposite sides of a parallelogram are parallel.

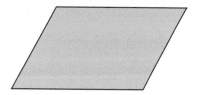

Only the opposite sides of a parallelogram are of equal length.
There are 4 angles in a parallelogram.

past

Time can be written using "past."

The time is 4:11.
It can also be written as 11 minutes past 4.

perimeter

The perimeter of a figure is the total length around it.

It can be measured in centimeters (cm), inches (in.), meters (m), and feet (ft).

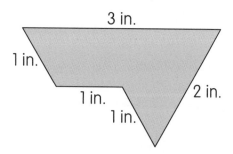

Perimeter of figure
= 3 + 2 + 1 + 1 + 1
= 8 in.

The perimeter of the figure is 8 inches.

- **perpendicular**

  Perpendicular lines are two lines that meet at a right angle.

  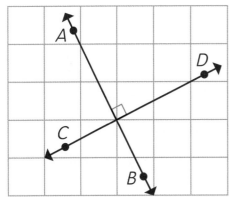

  Line *AB* is perpendicular to Line *CD*.

- **plane figure**

  Plane figures are flat figures. They may be open or closed.

- **point**

  A point is an exact location in space.

  Ȧ   This is Point *A*.

- **polygon**

  A polygon is a closed plane figure formed using three or more line segments.

- **rhombus**

  A rhombus is a quadrilateral. The opposite sides of a rhombus are parallel.

    All sides of a rhombus are of equal length.

  There are four angles in a rhombus.

- **right angle**

  A right angle is a special angle.

  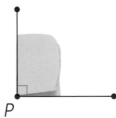

  Angle *P* is a right angle. Use the corner of the folded paper to check for a right angle.

- **square centimeter (cm²)**

  Square centimeter is a metric unit of measure for area. It is used for small areas.

  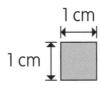

  This is a 1-centimeter square. Its area is 1 square centimeter (cm^2).

- **square foot (ft²)**

  Square foot is a customary unit of measure for area.
  It is used for large areas.

  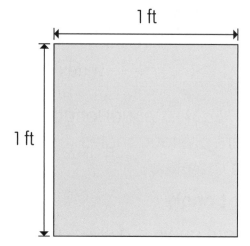
  1 ft

  1 ft

  A 1-foot square has an area of 1 square foot (ft²).

- **square inch (in²)**

  Square inch is a customary unit of measure for area.
  It is used for large areas.

  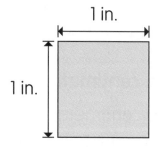
  1 in.

  1 in.

  This is a 1-inch square.
  Its area is 1 square inch (in²).

- **square meter (m²)**

  Square meter is a metric unit of measure for area.
  It is used for large areas.

  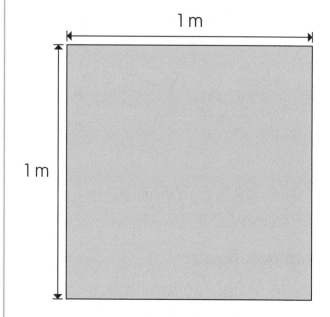
  1 m

  1 m

  A 1-meter square has an area of 1 square meter (m²).

- **square unit**

  Area is measured in square units such as square centimeters, square inches, square feet, and square meters.

T

- **timeline**

  A timeline can be drawn to find the start time, end time, or elapsed time of an activity.

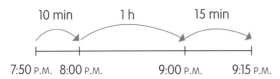

- **to**

  Time can be written using "to."

  The time is 7:54.
  It can also be written as 6 minutes to 8.

U

- **unit fraction**

  A unit fraction names one of the equal parts of a whole. Its numerator is 1.

  $\frac{1}{2}, \frac{1}{3}, \frac{1}{4}, \frac{1}{6}$, and $\frac{1}{8}$ are unit fractions.

V

- **vertex**

  Two sides of a polygon meet at a point called the vertex. An angle is formed at the vertex.

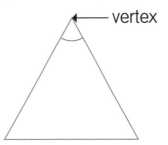

  vertex

- **volume**

  Volume is the amount of liquid in a container.

  The volume of water in the measuring jug is 60 milliliters.

W

- **whole**

  A fraction is part of a whole. All parts of a shape make up a whole.

  $\frac{2}{3}$ and $\frac{1}{3}$ make 1 whole.

Index

A

Angles, *throughout, see for example,* 347–352, 382, 387–388, 390–391, 394–395
    comparing
        to right angle, 352, 356–357, 362, 401
    identifying, 347–350
        in shapes, 344, 351
    making, 354

Area, **119**–172, 194–198, 201, 204–206, 208, *see also* Area model
    estimating, 124, 149
    of figure, *throughout, see for example,* 145–147, 155–156, 158–159, 195–198
        by separating rectangles, 163–164
    finding
        of rectangle using multiplication, 160–161, 163, 170
        in square centimeters, *see* Square centimeters (cm^2)
        in square feet, *see* Square feet (ft^2)
        in square inches, *see* Square inches (in^2)
        in square meters, *see* Square meters (m^2)
        using half-square units, 122–123, 125
        using square units, 119–125, 128, 129, 195

Area model
    multiplying using, 114

B

Balance scale
    pictorial representations, 66–67

Bar graphs, *throughout, see for example,* 112, 266, 283, 289–290, 292
    pictorial representations, *throughout, see for example,* 266, 283, 298, 302, 329
    from picture graphs, 284, 287
    solving problems using, 298, 300

Bar models, *throughout, see for example,* 18, 30, 34, 49, 54
    fractions as part of set using, 27–29
    pictorial representations, *throughout, see for example,* 22, 27–30, 49–50, 68, 90–92

C

Capacity, **81**, 87–88, 102–105
    measuring, 81–84

Centimeters (cm), *throughout, see for example,* 116, 118, 131, 155–156, 158

Clock, *throughout, see for example,* 212, 215–217, 220–221, 223, 252
    manipulative, 215, 218–219, 222, 225, 231

Closed plane figures, **380**–381
    identifying, 380, 402

Color number cubes, 297

Combine
    flat shapes to form other flat shapes, 341

Comparison
    angles to right angle, 352, 356–357, 362, 401
    fractions, 41–45, 47–48, 52

Connecting cubes, 25–27, 269

Conversion
    hours to minutes, 225–226, 254
    minutes to hours and minutes, 227, 254

Counting
    by 5s to tell time, 212
    flat shapes number of sides and corners, 340

Craft sticks, 350, 363, 383

Cubes
    color number, *see* Color number cubes
    connecting, *see* Connecting cubes

Curves, 338–339

Customary units
    measuring length using, 117

> Pages in **boldface** type show where a term is introduced.

real-world problems involving, 240, 243, 245
start, *see* Start time
telling, *see* Telling time

Timeline, *throughout, see for example,* 112, **231**, 233–234, 237, 239
    pictorial representations, 231–232, 234–239, 241–243, 245–246, 254

"To," **218**–221, 223–224, 255, 259
    telling time to nearest minute using, 218–220, 254

Transparent counters, 28

Trapezoids, *throughout, see for example,* 340, 342, 344, 352, 388

Unit fractions, **7**
    understanding, 52

Unit of measure, 80, 131, 135, 143, 147

Unit squares
    to estimate area, 149, 160

Vertex, *throughout, see for example,* **382**, 384, 386, 394, 400

Vertical axis, 285–286, 291

Volume, **77**–78, 91, 102
    of liquid, 84, 87, 103
    liters and milliliters, 85–86
    measure, 77, 80–81, 84, 102

Whole, **6**, 16–18, 21–24, 51, 55
    using fractions, parts of, 6–9, 13–15, 52

Whole numbers
    as fractions, 19, 46

Photo Credits

1: © Evgeniya Uvarova/Dreamstime.com,
1t: © dreamerb/123rf.com, 19t: © kosam/Shutter Stock, 19m: © Africa Studio/Shutter Stock, 19b: © Kia Cheng Boon/123rf.com, 20: © piotr_pabijan/Shutter Stock, 24: © belchonock/123rf.com, 25m: © MCE. Objects sponsored by Noble International Pte Ltd., 25b: © Kydriashka/Dreamstime.com, 26l: © Kydriashka/Dreamstime.com, 26r: © MCE. Objects sponsored by Noble International Pte Ltd., 27t: © MCE. Objects sponsored by Noble International Pte Ltd., 27m: © Anton Samsonov/123rf.com, 28: © MCE, 35: © Aimee M Lee/Shutter Stock, 45: © piotr_pabijan/Shutter Stock, 49: Created by Fwstudio – Freepik.com, 49b: © Todja/Shutter Stock, 50: © olegdudko/123rf.com, 51: © Piliphoto/Dreamstime.com, 59: © Natthawut Panyosaeng/123rf.com, 60: © karandaev/123rf.com, 61: © eyewave/123rf.com, 62: © Elnur/iStock, 64: © Zoia Lukianova/123rf.com, 64tr: © Bluelela/Dreamstime.com, 64br: © targovcom/iStock, 65t: © Sergey Sukhanov/123rf.com, 65m: © PICONEST/Shutter Stock, 65tl: © 123rfaurinko/123rf.com, 65tr: © Serfii Kucher/123rf.com, 65b: © Pannawat Muangmoon/123rf.com, 65b: © PICONEST/Shutter Stock, 65bl: © lucadp/123rf.com, 65br: © Kidsada Manchinda/123rf.com, 66tl: © Jamakosy/iStock, 66tr: © area381/Shutter Stock, 66bl: © Andregric/iStock, 67t: © Timmary/123rf.com, 67m: © Hyrman/Dreamstime.com, 67b: © Mikhail Kokhanchikov/Dreamstime.com, 69m: © Maksym Narodenko/123rf.com, 69b: © Natalyka/Dreamstime.com, 70t: © George Tsartsianidis/123rf.com, 70m: © Natthapon Ngamnithiporn/123rf.com, 70b: © Evan Lorne/Shutter Stock, 71tr: © karandaev/123rf.com, 71ml: © klotz/123rf.com, 71ml: © pogonici/123rf.com, 71bl: © Dingalt/Dreamstime.com, 72t: © Infinity T29/Shutter Stock, 72b: © Jiri Miklo/123rf.com, 73t: © Airborne77/Dreamstime.com, 73m: © Diana Taliun/123rf.com, 73b: © Benjamin Simeneta/123rf.com, 74t: © Georgii Dolgykh/123rf.com, 74b: © Oleksii Terpugov/Dreamstime.com, 75t: © Olga Popova/123rf.com, 75m: © MARGRIT HIRSCH/Shutter Stock, 75b: © Anton Starikov/123rf.com, 76(t to b): i) © Antonio Gravante/123rf.com, ii) © siraphol/123rf.com, iii) © pixelbliss/123rf.com, iv) © Alexey Yuminov/123rf.com, 77t: © Anton Starikov/123rf.com, 77b(l to r): i) © Boris Fedorenko/123rf.com, ii) kornienko/123rf.com, iii) © avesun/123rf.com, iv) © kornienko/123rf.com, 78t: © George Tsartsianidis/123rf.com, 78bl: © MCE,

78br: © MCE, 80tl: © gresei/123rf.com, 80tr: © Mariusz Blach/123rf.com, 80bl: © Igor Tarasyuk/123rf.com, 80br: © Veniamin Kraskov/123rf.com, 81: © Prapan Ngawkeaw/123rf.com, 82t: © Mariyana M/Shutter Stock, 82b: © photoshkolnik/123rf.com, 83t(l to r): i) © Todsaporn Bunmuen/Dreamstime.com, ii) © Mm88/Dreamstime.com, iii) © Nikola Spasenoski/Dreamstime.com, iv) © Banepx/Dreamstime.com, 83b(l to r): i) © Martin Damen/123rf.com, ii) © Cipariss/Dreamstime.com, iii) © Eutoch/Dreamstime.com, iv) © Tasakorn Kongmoon/Dreamstime.com, 84t: © Petro Korchmar/Dreamstime.com, 84bl: © Danny Smythe/123rf.com, 84br: © George Tsartsianidis/123rf.com, 86t: © Alexey Kolotvin/123rf.com, 86m: © Anton Starikovdreamerb/123rf.com, 86b: © magraphicsdreamerb/123rf.com, 87: © Viktoriya Chursina/123rf.com, 88t: © Kitch Bain/123rf.com, 88m: © Iryna Bort/123rf.com, 88b: © heinteh/123rf.com, 91: © shutswis/123rf.com, 94: © piotr_pabijan/Shutter Stock, 95l: © serezniy/123rf.com, 95r: © Chernetskaya/Dreamstime.com, 97: © belchonock/123rf.com, 98l: © Kidsada Manchinda/123rf.com, 98r: © siraphol/123rf.com, 99: Created by Fwstudio – Freepik.com, 102tl: © Oleksii Terpugov/123rf.com, 102tr: © serezniy/123rf.com, 102bl: © Edward Westmacott/123rf.com, 102br: © Olga Kovalenko/123rf.com, 103tl: © Beautyoflife13/Dreamstime.com, 103tr: © boumenjapet/123rf.com, 103b: © Alexandr Kornienko/Dreamstime.com, 104: © andersonrise/123rf.com, 107l: © Parinya Binsuk/123rf.com, 107r: © Bohuslav Jelen/123rf.com, 108: © Sergii Gnatiuk/Dreamstime.com, 109: © pioneer111/iStock, 110: © ClaudioVentrella/iStock, 112t: © Andrey Armyagov/123rf.com, 112m: © Iurii Kovalenko/123rf.com, 112b: © 3DSculptor/iStock, 113: © Stanisic Vladimir/123rf.com, 113t: © Keren Woodgyer/123rf.com, 113b: © QinJin/Shutter Stock, 117: © Mike Flippo/123rf.com, 143: © MikeRickword/iStock, 144: © Weerapat Kiatdumrong/123rf.com, 147: © Alexey Bykov/123rf.com, 147tl: © Alexey Bykov, 147tr: © Oleksandr Kulichenko/123rf.com, 155: © Eshma/iStock, 160: © Rose Waddell/123rf.com, 178: © Shlomo Polonsky/123rf.com, 189: © Epitavi/iStock, 191: Created by Fwstudio – Freepik.com, 193: © belchonock/123rf.com, 207: © Filip Fuxa/123rf.com, 208b: © ewastudio/123rf.com, 208br: © Mike Flippo/123rf.com, 209b: © ewastudio/123rf.com, 209br: © kurhan/123rf.com, 211: © Ventura69/iStock, 211tr: © rangizzz/123rf.com,

© 2020 Marshall Cavendish Education Pte Ltd

Published by Marshall Cavendish Education
Times Centre, 1 New Industrial Road, Singapore 536196
Customer Service Hotline: (65) 6213 9688
US Office Tel: (1-914) 332 8888 | Fax: (1-914) 332 8882
E-mail: cs@mceducation.com
Website: www.mceducation.com

Distributed by
Houghton Mifflin Harcourt
125 High Street
Boston, MA 02110
Tel: 617-351-5000
Website: www.hmhco.com/programs/math-in-focus

First published 2020

ISBN 978-0-358-10183-3

Printed in Singapore

5 6 7 8 9 10   1401   26 25 24 23 22
4500839423   B C D E F

The cover image shows a llama.
Llamas live in herds on the mountains of South America.
A baby llama is called a cria.
Like horses and donkeys, llamas are often used to transport goods.
Llamas are intelligent animals and they can learn simple tasks or instructions quickly.
Their soft wool can be used to make warm clothes like scarves and sweaters.